BE

HEROICS

BEYOND
HEROICS

LIVING
OUR
MYTHS

MADELINE L. MCMURRAY, PH.D.

Nicolas-Hays
York Beach, Maine

First published in 1995 by
Nicolas-Hays, Inc.
P. O. Box 612
York Beach, ME 03910-0612

Distributed to the trade by
Samuel Weiser, Inc.
P. O. Box 612
York Beach, ME 03910-0612

Library of Congress Cataloging-in-Publication Data
McMurray, Madeline
    Beyond heroics : living our myths / by Madeline
    McMurray.
        p.   cm.
    Includes bibliographical references and index.
    1. Attitude   (Psychology)   2. Mythology—Psycho-
logical aspects.   3. Adaptability (Psychology)   4. Self.
I. Title.
BF327.M37   1995
291.1'3—dc20   95-10679
                                                    CIP
ISBN 0-89254-031-1
BJ

Cover design by Ed Stevens

Typeset in 11 point Palatino

Printed in the United States of America
01   00   99   98   97   96   95
10   9   8   7   6   5   4   3   2   1

The paper used in this publication meets the minimum
requirements of the American National Standard for Perma-
nence of Paper for Printed Library Materials Z39.48-1984.

I dedicate this book to David McMurray—my best friend. Thank you for being both a challenging and supporting partner in the mythic life we share.

TABLE OF CONTENTS

FOREWORD

by
Stephen Aizenstat, Ph.D.

As persons and as a species, we are asked to discover, or perhaps *recover*, a way of knowing and a way of living that moves beyond the prevailing heroic attitude. This attitude, an attitude of domination and power over our planet, divorces humankind from the cycles of nature. This separation creates disruption and disharmony between the restorative processes of nature and the generative push of the human species. What results is environmental catastrophe and social deprivation. Of course, this news is not new; yet we humans forge ahead, strong-willed, confident, and seemingly determined to deny our interdependence with the "others"—the things and creatures with whom we share the planet. Our attitudes and behaviors are well-entrenched and quite forceful: we *will* succeed; we *will* conquer this land.

However, if we continue living the heroic myth—simply using the world as if it is exclusively ours—we will, in turn, destroy "our" world. As the millennium draws near, we humans must come to recognize that we are participants in a complex, interrelated web of being. Ocean, desert, forest, sky, animals, plants, stones, and human beings are all constituent members of community earth—all interrelated ecosystems, each vital to the survival and sustainability of the others. To discover or, more accurately, to *re-discover* this "interactive" and "interdependent" worldview requires, I believe, a reconsideration of our

xii / MADELINE MCMURRAY

essential beliefs about the relationship between persons and planet.

Psychologists tell us that to change behavior one must first change the attitude that creates it. Yet, even before the attitude, there is something else: a belief system that in fundamental ways evokes that attitude—a belief system that has shaped our feelings, structured our thinking, and oriented the very assumptions we have made (and continue to make) about living in this world. This belief system is passed from one person to the next and is perpetuated through and supported by our culture. It is displayed in the symbols of our time and embodied in the structures and monuments that surround us. These shared beliefs are the *mythologies* that govern our very being, that teach us our values, that spell out our ethical codes. Our mythologies underpin our attitudes and, thus, our behavior toward everything around us. Our mythologies, whatever they may be, therefore, are basic to our relationship to planet Earth.

Consider for a moment, the myth of "manifest destiny." Implied in that myth, that system of belief, is an entitlement to land and ownership of that land. It is our god-given right, our destiny, says this myth, to lay claim to more and more land—to call it ours and to do with it whatever might serve our needs and desires. Natural consequences of this belief, of living this myth, are clear-cutting forests, strip-mining mountains, replanting prairies for the benefit of humankind, dislocating animal populations from their natural habitats, and even exterminating species of plants and animals as humans follow their "destiny." These actions seem expedient—in the short run however, they ignore future ramifications. Acts that are short-sighted and person-centered alienate the sympathetic relationship between the landscape and that which is fundamental to our mutual future survival.

We are in need of a new myth, a new way of thinking mythically, an expanded, interrelational point of view. Only if we begin to live such a new myth will our actions change toward the others with whom we share the planet. We need to develop a way of living that *joins with* the creatures, plants, elements, and things of the world rather than separating from them. We must learn to differentiate without separation. Just as our psychology must change from an ego-centered view of psyche to an *eco*-centered perspective, so, too, must our mythology shift from a monotheistic, heroic story to a polytheistic tale of relationship. Our *experience* of mythology must transform as well. No longer can we view mythology as a fixed story, experienced in the statis language of an oft-repeated narrative. We must experience mythology as a living dimension of our psychic reality. We must interact with the images of myth as vital, embodied constituents of our living mythic ecology. Our relationship to the stories of myth must change, even as the stories themselves must be different.

Our new mythology is not really new at all. It is not a newly developed system of ideas which we invent, or a "new" cosmology that is uncovered/rediscovered by archaeologists. It need not appear as a "lost" text or a newly-inspired sermon. Rather, the new myth is here now. It lives within us as a vital force, as alive as we are. It is generative, a wellspring of creative life, an underground river flowing beneath the surface of observable life. Each of us has access to this ever-present mythic realm. The new myth is new only in our awareness of it. It lives in the "inscape" of all beings—here, now, always behind, beneath, around the visible. It is nature's soul life, her resonant presence. Her way. Her pulse—always pushing.

Our culture yearns for soul—care of the soul, soul-making, soul in the world, soul mates, modern man in search of soul. What is it that we yearn for and cannot find? Perhaps it is a way of being in the world: a way of being that is mythologically connected to the gods and goddesses, the spirits, of an animated world. To notice the presence of these invisibles requires taking the time to listen—to surrender control and to engage with the poetic life, the rhythm ever-present in the songs of all beings and all things. The world of myth is alive each moment in an alive world. In this world alive with psychic vibrancy, it is we who must develop our capacity to hear the mythic language of the world. It is we who are inside a mythology, not a mythology that is inside of us. To listen mythically, then, is be a part of the very myth that, in turn, helps shape who we are and who we are becoming.

How do we hear our mythological stirrings and live mythically in the world? First, we realize that the language of soul is metaphor—soul speaks in the poetic of myth. To listen to the world speaking is to hear the poem at its heart. To live mythically is to open ourselves to the poetic basis of experience.

Second, to experience life mythically is to live in the world interactively—in relationship with all other beings. For example, to interact mythically with a flower is not only to witness it, to name it, or to appreciate its beauty. It is also to give back to that flower, to tend that flower. To be in the world in a way that offers something back is to live mythically. The flower does not exist merely for our enjoyment of its beauty. Rather, the flower seeks out, it draws us to it, perhaps to ask for something in return. From an eco-mythological point of view, the flower wants, needs our attention. Our gaze helps sustain it. Mindful attending is a way we can give back to the world, ensoul the world. When we interact mythically, we participate in the creation of the soul body of our planet.

A third way to experience life mythically is to live in the world as if it were a dream. When we are living within this perspective, everything is dreaming—the stones, the trees, the buildings, the animals. Stories are being told by every thing, each in its own language. Each creature and thing speaks in its own voice, and the world is alive with sounds and stories. The worldscape is a dreamscape, and we are but one part of Earth's dream. Learning and practicing ways of tending our dreams connects us to the realm of the world dreaming and to the mythic way of knowing which lives in the souls of all beings and things.

We are being asked to try on this new way of living in the world. Live mythically, as if our myth is our heart, our soul, our skin. Learn and live this way of being in the world. Recognize the life pulse inherent in all of us—people, creatures, trees, rocks, sand grains, dandelion puffs, volcanoes—all of us who dwell in our world, as well as on the planet. Our world is asking us to find the stories and the tools—the myths—that will help us live mythically. In *Beyond Heroics: Living Our Myths*, Madeline McMurray responds to this plea with reflections, teachings, and exercises that foster a way of living mythically. We are called upon to practice this way of living in our world so that she and we will survive.

ACKNOWLEDGMENTS

Although I have authored this book it is, in truth, a product that involves an entire community of people. I want to say "thank you" to each of those people who helped in the creation of this book: Ellen Gibb-Moore and Raphaelle Butler for working with me on my dissertation, forming the foundational research that came before the writing; Matina Kilkenny for working through the rough ideas and outlines that created the first draft; Charlie DiCostanzo and Meinrad Craighead for their calm participation; my sister, Pat Wheeler, for her affirming attitude over the last two years of putting the manuscript together; friends who read the text at all different levels of development: Lesley Meriwether, Harry Blumenthal, Stephen Aizenstat, and Richard Duning. My patient partner, David, who listened to all the shaky parts in quiet morning hours and listened, just one more time, at the end of a work-filled day. I have also been helped in this project by the people I meet every day in the classroom and the consulting room. They, too, are an important part of my community. In fact, they are the fabric of this book. I give a special thanks to all those clients and students who shared their myths with me. Also, I feel gratitude to the myths and stories that have woven themselves together in this creation, as well as the presentations from the "dreamtime."

Ultimately, the decision to save the environment must come from the human heart.

—the 14th Dalai Lama

PREFACE

Individually and collectively, we are dominated by a mythology of being number one, of being "king of the mountain" and of being right. As a psychotherapist and a teacher, I am acutely aware of people's demand for answers—even incorrect answers. Students want to be told what to think rather than to meet the challenge of learning how to think. Clients want a magic pill to make the turmoil of their lives disappear. We all prefer the security of having the "right" answer over the task of learning to tolerate the tension of difference and conflict. Unfortunately, when comfort is our standard, change is not the outcome. Clinging to already preconceived answers leads to repeating empty patterns. Developing one's capacity to stay in the confusion of not knowing is often the pathway to new perceptions that enable growth and expansion. Tolerating the unknown is key to finding insights that lead to new behaviors.

We are in a time of transition—a time of millennial change. As we envision the possibilities of remythologizing our world, we need to be open to that which has not yet come into being. The answers of the past are not necessarily applicable to the future. We must acknowledge the turmoil of our times and live within its discomfort. Through facing the no longer effective behaviors of our collective, we begin to sense some of the ingredients for a healthier future. We are a society focused too long on mythologies of the individual and the heroic-warrior-king. We have yet to discover and recover myths that enable future becoming.

Wrestling with the problem—not providing the answer—is the primary intention of this text. A variety of possible solutions are offered within these pages. Each chapter examines a mythic approach that either challenges our concept of the hero, or moves to mythologies that are non-heroic. This lack of clearly concluded answers, to complex futuristic questions, is likely to disturb readers. Still, the challenge of living with the tension of the questions is our best response for now. In fact, tolerance of ambiguity may be part of the solution. We can't be certain which myths will be most important in the formation of a worldview that meets the needs of the 21st century. It is not my intent to prioritize myths, or to encourage following one mythic theme over another. On the other hand, I am not building a case that just any old myth will do. What I am suggesting is a mythic framework by which we question and evaluate the myths we live.

The guidelines of this book are: (1) The dominant heroic mythology of the Western world is a partial development comparable to adolescent and early adult stages of life. (2) We have yet to achieve a level that includes our collective soul. (3) It is important to explore our myths for more than personal expansion. (4) Remythologizing the future will include a return to sacred mythology. (5) Mythologies that support and nourish diversity are essential for our personal and collective wholeness.

Myths for the future must have outcomes that transform our present heroic-warrior-king mythology into a mythic structure where the sacredness of life is the central theme; the wisdom of the ages is reintegrated into consciousness; anthropocentricism is put behind us; the feminine creative principle is once again valued; human balance in relationship to the rest of creation is retrieved and our commonality as human beings is central. This book is clearly not an exhaustive study. It is a beginning step; speculating on myths that might keep the human species a viable option in planetary survival. The myths we live will determine our outcome.

CHAPTER ONE

MYTHOLOGY AND THE TRANSPERSONAL

As we move uncertainly toward the end of the 20th century and anticipate the beginning of the 21st, our shifting awareness searches for paradigms, guidelines, and models for the future. We are awkwardly piecing together the puzzle: the disintegration of the world we have known and a reintegration, a re-creation, of a world that is coming into being. Nothing is stable, nothing secure. We are excited and unnerved by the perpetual motion of world events. It is the mythic dimension in the world (as well as within the psyche of each of us) that enables stability to exist within instability. As the world changes so do we. As we change so does the world. All life continually disintegrates and reintegrates in the archetypal pattern of death-rebirth.

For centuries the primary mythology of the European-American framework has been the hero/warrior/king.[1] In our politics, our relationships, our religion, and our psychology we have placed this heroic warrior-king at the center. Through concern for gender issues, this model is presently being augmented to include the feminine aspects of heroics and power. Redefinition is only the beginning. Feminine consciousness requires a psychological development that is much more expansive than simply placing a female figurehead on the throne.

In the development of modern psychology, this mythic theme of heroics—defined here as ego development—has subjugated other possibilities of personality maturation. It is time to reexamine the hero's journey and expand upon

---

[1]Joseph Campbell, *The Hero With A Thousand Faces*, Bollingen Series XVII (Princeton, NJ: Princeton University Press, 1949, 1968).

the possibilities, not only within that particular framework, but beyond heroics. Joseph Henderson, writing on the archetype of the hero in *Man and His Symbols*, describes heroic development as a movement toward further growth. He says:

> Once the individual has passed his initial test and can enter the mature phase of life, the hero myth loses its relevance. The hero's symbolic death becomes, as it were, the achievement of that maturity.[2]

Within human personality there is another journey to be taken, a journey that moves us beyond the heroic ego toward a development of soul. In depth psychology there are two forms of consciousness standing side by side within every person: one focused, one diffuse; one linear, one cyclical; one yin, one yang; one related to ego, one connected to soul. These two movements can be described as personal and transpersonal, or as ego and archetype.

As a psychotherapist, I witness the movement beyond the hero in what the therapeutic community commonly calls "midlife" clients. Generally, midlife issues cluster somewhere around the 40- to 60-year-old individual. Although most of my work is oriented to that group, midlife is more accurately an intermediate level of adult development not dependent upon having achieved one's 40th birthday nor limited by already having reached one's 60th. Age is not the determining factor for psychological growth. The formation of personality seems a combination of life experiences and the ability to develop reflective consciousness.

The hero, as a psychological stage, germinates in adolescents with the formation of the identity by which we

---

[2]Joseph Henderson, "Ancient Myths and Modern Man," in C. G. Jung, *Man and His Symbols* (Garden City: Doubleday, 1964), p. 104.

begin to newly define ourselves and our place in the world. We try to make clear who we are, what we are about and what choices we want to make. The ego structure of our personality is increased and redefined. Choices propel us into new relationships, new thinking, new philosophies. We begin a career, we compete, conquer, win, lose, take our stands, overcome our dragons and eventually make a workable, sometimes even satisfying, life.

Then come the middle years. Midlife has become known for turmoil and crisis. We are meant to embrace soul-work rather than continuing to receive rewards through heroic achievements. Attachments to earlier heroic deeds block future becoming. To remain in the once-successful heroic model keeps us tied to repetitive patterns that grind us down and block our deepening into soul.

If, as individuals and as a culture, we stagnate in the mythology of heroics, we will probably fall short of the demands of our rapidly changing world. The egoic hero as the center of personality, or the center of society, limits the wisdom of a more expansive development. When individual actions are without soul, the consequences are a world without spirit, without depth, without meaning.

Modern seekers of psychological enlightenment are very aware of mythology. The goddesses of virgin, mother, and crone have begun to sound like personality types. The archetype of the wildwoman howls through women's groups, while the warrior and the wildman are central to the blossoming men's movement. Our present psychological perspective on mythology directs itself toward personal awareness, penetrating into who and why we are. A less developed—but no less significant—view provides recognition of the individual's relationship to the collective. Important insights present themselves when the language and images of myths are used to examine an individual life. But personal interpretations of mythology without the dimension of a cultural perspective restrict the larger intention of myth.

When I work with clients in therapy, or students in the classroom, I find an intense fascination with mythology. I also see that learning to apply myths and fairy tales to one's daily life—seeing that life in the context of a larger social and spiritual order—is a bit like learning a foreign language. Mythology is a language we have yet to master. To expand into the spiritual-social dimension of mythology involves guidelines for understanding myths beyond the limits of subjectivity. Before myth became individualized through psychology it was collective in its purposes. It is essential that this collective dimension be restored so that the individual might better find his/her place in the whole. Our prevalent mythology of the individual as the whole, or at least the center of the whole, has brought us to the point of possible extinction.

The attempt to understand myths psychologically is a major contribution to our modern thinking about human behavior. Much of this book is influenced by a psychological analysis of myth, as well as by my personal bias toward archetypal psychology. Nonetheless, it is critical to address the psychological hubris of putting the human at the center, to secure the spiritual and communal significance of mythology. Mythology has an integrity of its own that includes a purpose that transcends the personal.[3] Myths are guides for the individual within the communal body of society as well as guardians of the knowledge of our larger metaphysical possibilities.

Most of you who are drawn to this book are familiar with the idea of mythology as something observable in human behavior. You can probably appreciate what a woman means when she explains herself as operating out of an inner "Aphrodite" in her repeated love affairs, or what a man implies when he says that he is expressing his "warrior" behavior in his competitive professional life.

---

[3]Joseph Campbell, *Myths to Live By* (New York: Bantam, 1988), pp. 13, 22–23.

These are personal interpretations (of mythic patterns within individual behavior) that are valid and useful. You might, however, be less conscious of the mythic connection to a transpersonal reality, to sacred time, to sacramental living or to deeper spiritual potentials.[4] If myths are to complete their function of connecting the human to the more transcendent realities of nature and the universe, we must include the transpersonal dimension—the invisible behind the visible—in our mythic development.

The neglect of the sacred function of myth, as well as excessive psychological interpretation, has led to seeing the heroic individual as the center of mythic development. We mistakenly believe that once the hero are in place we are set. We see the hero's journey as a goal rather than a process leading to other things—things not yet known. There is a lack of awareness of further development. The anthropocentric mythology of the last few centuries reveals itself today in endlessly egocentric attitudes of excess, greed, and power. Power struggles between nations, between communities, and between species, are the outcome of a mythology that places the heroic individual at the center. As mythmakers, it is imperative that we retrieve authority for ourselves and for the social order from the hands of the warrior-kings and return to a mythology where dominion lies in the realm of the gods and goddesses. Guidance for living must come, as it once did, from the mythic models of the celestial archetypes and their divine energies. Myth, by its very definition, is meant to expand out to our environment, to our community, to our past, to our future, to our planet, and to our universe.

---

[4]Mircea Eliade, "Patterns in Comparative Religion," in *Transformations of Myth through Time*, Eisenberg et al, eds. (Orlando: Harcourt Brace, 1990), pp. 15–26; *The Myth of the Eternal Return*, Bollingen Series XLVI (Princeton, NJ: Princeton University Press, 1954); *The Sacred and the Profane* (New York: Harcourt Brace, 1957).

A MYTHIC VIEW

Myths are legends, stories, fairytales, sacred literature, and religious teachings. There are modern myths as well as ancient; living myths as well as those that have passed away. At the simplest level, everything that is lived in the world is someone's myth. We each have myths that influence and guide our lives. We have social myths about God and country, about money, materialism, and success; we have family myths about relationship and power; and we have personal myths about who we can and cannot be. Being aware of the particular myth that creates the framework for our life provides us with more knowledge of self, family, and community. Our myths are our world view, our ideas, and our actions.

To search for an understanding of mythology, you must begin by looking directly into the activity of your own life. Myth lies just below the surface of behavior. I often ask students and clients to write about the myths that guide their lives. We each have mythic patterns transmitted to us by family, community, friends, society. These are so automatic and ingrained that we are unconscious of their mythic influence. You don't generally think of your daily life as mythic behavior, but it is. You might go to work every day because you believe in the American mythology of hard work as a value. On the other hand, your desire to work could be driven by a mythology of status or material gain. You might give charitable contributions because of some basic religious ideation of taking care of others, or it could be your way of belonging to a particular social organization. Actions are motivated by mythological ideations. The guidelines for making daily choices are the myths we live by.

EXERCISE 1

EXPLORING YOUR MYTH

Before going further, it may be helpful to take time to explore your own myth. We each need to become aware of the mythology that guides our choices. Begin by making a list of labels that you would use to describe yourself to another person. For example:

> I am a Buddhist;
> I am a student;
> I am a dedicated parent;
> I am a manager of a business;
> I am a republican.

Now make a brief outline of your weekly or monthly activities. Take an inventory of how you spend your time and why you are doing what you do. For example:

I.   WORK
    A. What you do—think about the specifics of your job.
    B. How many hours do you spend at work?
    C. What are the rewards of your work?
    D. What do you do before and after work?
    E. Why do you do these things (For example, if you ride your bike to and from work, is it because you want the exercise? or because of concern for the environment? etc.)

II. LEISURE TIME
    A. What you do—hobbies, family time, volunteer time, friends, exercise, etc.
    B. How many hours do you spend with each thing you've listed.
    C. What are the rewards of each activity?

When you have listed your activities, do the same thing with your bank account. Look at how you spend your money. For example:

I. HOUSEHOLD
    A. Essentials (by your definition)
    B. Choices
II. DONATIONS
III. ENTERTAINMENT
IV. ETC.

Between your self-definition and how you spend your time and money you will begin to discern your particular living myth. To expand your mythic awareness further, reflect upon how you might have developed the guiding beliefs you listed earlier. For example: "I am a republican because my parents were both republicans." Or, "I am a Buddhist because I had to find something more meaningful than the atheism of my background."

As a final step, take the information that you have outlined and write a paragraph on the four or five points that have the most meaning to you, i.e., those things that you give the most personal value.

The formation of our mythology began long ago. Generations back in time, when our ancestors traveled across uncharted territory to establish new homes in unknown lands, our personal history was in the making. Our background of family and culture, along with our particular personal experiences, have brought each of us to where we stand today.

Had not my great-great grandparents embarked from Wales and reached what is now called the state of Virginia, had not the next generation crossed a still wild land, I might never have come to know the wonders and the terrors of the "American Dream" that I am living today. Similarly, had not my Cambodian student been granted parents and grandparents strong enough to endure the losses of home and country and the capacity to begin again in a foreign land, he and I would not be in this Dream together. We stand here today, in our roles of student and teacher, not only because of our individual efforts, but because of all those who dared to travel this road before us.

The mythic dimensions of our lives are a crude combination of past and present. This mythic dimension is a dynamic mystery still weaving itself toward the future. Today's challenge is to live the individual and collective mythology that best enables the human species to exist within the framework of planetary generativity. Human evolution is unusually slow compared to the geranium and the average housefly. We lack the genetic ability to make environmental adaptations in one quick generation. If our air becomes unbreathable, we'll cease to breathe; if our water becomes undrinkable, we won't have time to learn to do without it. We will not be an easy species to salvage from the endangered list. We humans are much more fragile than we dare to examine. Yet the greatest strength within our grasp might be the quality of imagination and the spirit that generates mythology. It is our nature to be mythmakers, and it is the nature of myth to encounter the issues of life and death. Myths and rituals are the ever-changing framework through which the human being can best meet the demands of ongoing adaptation.

COLLECTIVE CONNECTIONS

All collective bodies have myths and rituals that preserve their continuity. We have as many mythologies as we have varieties of cultures and people on this planet. Between communication technology and population migrations we are experiencing the greatest mixing of mythologies that has ever occurred in the development of the human species. When mythic systems meet, there is often little tolerance for differences. Historically, "assimilate or perish" has been the rule. Technology provides us with international communication, but not international relatedness. Time and time again, mythologies clash and the strongest—not always the wisest—dominates. History enshrines the mythology that wins the greatest number of battles and holds the most political and material power.

We stand today in a world that is beginning to challenge the adequacy of a myth that only works for the "winners." The idea of Planet Earth as a global village is bringing into our awareness the need for an expanded mythology that can embrace diversity. The postmodern world may need to cease doing battle and begin to encourage variations in mythic themes. Pluralism and diversity are part of the paradigm for the future. Myths that enable us to respond to conflicts through acceptance of difference, while looking for our shared connection, are essential to the growing complexity of our world.

Can the mythology of the warrior continue to meet the needs of a world in environmental crisis? Is war our most effective method for dealing with the planetary issue of over-population? Is the heroic always the best stance to take in facing our present social and political issues? What are the results of the war on drugs, the war on poverty, wars between nations, wars between states, wars between communities? Does changing the warrior to one who follows a spiritual path make a difference? What might some other possibilities begin to look like?

The myths we believe in perpetuate and create the world in which we live. Myths are not the untruths of an age but the deeper truths, the truths that determine the choices that we make. As long as the warrior remains our primary mythic figure, we will choose, time and time again, to meet our needs through the tools of war and dominance. Mythologies that continue to keep people and cultures enemies, rather than creating new relationships, keep us forever locked in ongoing cycles of power and destruction.

REDISCOVERING THE POWER OF MYTH

As we rediscover the substance of our mythologies we begin to weave them into the context of the modern world. We can consciously choose the myths that best meet the needs of the future, rather than unconsciously living patterns that lead to further destruction of life here on Earth. As the planet grows more and more crowded, we will need to rediscover and reinterpret mythologies that support the greatest amount of diversity. Not only diversity of peoples, but diversity of all species, and of all things animate and inanimate. We have yet to weave together the tapestry of a global view. We have yet to learn the myths whose heart would bring relatedness into being. A starting point for learning the importance of heart is in this Ugandan myth titled "The Creation of the World."

> Kabezya-Mpungu, the highest god, had created the sky and the earth and two human beings, a man and a woman, endowed with Reason. However, these two human beings did not, as yet possess Mutima, or Heart.[5]

Creation myths explain why things are the way they are. They remind us of our earlier development, and point to

---

[5]The story here, and on the following page, is from C. and W. Leslau, eds., "The Creation of the World," in *African Folktales* (White Plains, NY: Peter Pauper Press, 1963), pp. 5–6.

divine involvement as part of the human condition. In this story we are the human creation endowed with Reason but not yet possessing Heart, or Mutima.

> Kabezya-Mpungu had four children, the Sun, the Moon, Darkness, and Rain. He called them all together and said to them, "I want to withdraw now, so that Man can no longer see me. I will send down Mutima in my place, but before I take leave I want to know what you, Rain, are going to do." "Oh," replied Rain, "I think I'll pour down without cease and put everything under water." "No," answered the god, "don't do that! Look at these two," and he pointed to the man and the woman; "do you think they can live under water? You'd better take turns with the Sun. After you have sufficiently watered the earth, let the Sun go to work and dry it."
>
> "And how are you going to conduct yourself?" the god asked the Sun. "I intend to shine hotly and burn everything under me," said his second child.
>
> "No," replied Kabezya-Mpungu. "That cannot be. How do you expect the people whom I created to get food? When you have warmed the earth for a while, give Rain a chance to refresh it and make the fruit grow."
>
> "And you, Darkness, what are your plans?"
>
> "I intend to rule forever!" was the answer.
>
> "Have pity," cried the god. "Do you want to condemn my creatures, the lions, the tigers, and the serpents, to see nothing of the world I made? Listen to me: give the Moon time to shine on the earth, and when you see the Moon in its last quarter, then you may again rule."
>
> "But I have lingered too long; now I must go." And he disappeared.

Somewhat later, Mutima, Heart, came along, in a small container no bigger than a hand.

Heart was crying, and asked Sun, Moon, Darkness, and Rain, "Where is Kabezya-Mpungu, our father?"

"Father is gone," they said, "and we do not know where."

"Oh, how great is my desire," replied Heart, "to commune with him. But since I cannot find him I will enter into Man, and through him I will seek God from generation to generation."

And that is what happened. Ever since, all children born of Man contain Mutima, a longing for God.

From this mythic perspective our task is to follow the heart within us, the heart that longs for God. The story informs us that we are born with the longing for God and that it is our natural impulse to seek relationship to the creator. The myth also shows us that there is an impulse in each of God's children to seek dominance and power. The sun wants to shine fully and the rain wants to rain abundantly. Each element in the story—Sun, Moon, Darkness, and Rain—desires dominance. The creator-god reminds us that creation is to be enjoyed by all. In this tale we hear an important message about relationships in nature, as well as about the true nature of the human heart.

EXERCISE 2

DISCOVERING HEART

1. Sit quietly and listen to the beat of your own heart. Let the image of heart fill your mind. Breathe deeply, relax, and think and feel HEART.

Figure 1. A wooden dance mask reminds us of the heart that yearns for the divine. From Geoffrey Williams, *African Designs from Traditional Sources* (New York: Dover, 1971), p. 125.

2. Look into your own heart and see what you can discover about yourself. How does your heart feel? What does it hold?

3. Make a brief list of words that describe your heart.

4. In the next twenty-four hours make a point of bringing this heart awareness into at least four situations in your daily life. For example, listen to the morning news with heart rather than reason.

Note: We have yet to find the conversion of heart that brings about an expansive mythology of common bonds, not only with the divine creator, but with all of creation. Unfortunately these matters of heart have too often had the divinity stripped away. We too easily turn to reason while sacrificing heart. Do we listen with heart when environmentalists tell us that we have only a few years to turn around our destruction of the Earth; or Aboriginal peoples say that they cannot sustain their ancient way of life on this planet?

Heart and soul were lost long ago while reason and logic won the day. Psychology and the social services have boiled human behavior down to intellectual interpretations and cookbook manuals for treatment plans. Terms like dysfunctional family, co-dependence, and addictions to anything and everything dominate our descriptions of what people are about. The same is true in the field of religion. The keepers of the faiths are not doing much better than the psychologists in matters of heart and soul. Literal interpretations of biblical mythology and assurances that faith will be enough do not offer adequate guidance in a world of overwhelming complexity.

When we turn to self-reflection, we often tend to either believe in a psychological framework, where we generate our own wellness, our own illness, our successes and our failures; or in a religious framework, where we can do nothing about our human condition. Either we are the warrior-king or God stands in for us in the same role. Even when we make God a woman, we want to slip her into the same position of power. Having broken the bonds of "superstition" (which might have been intuition) we have unfortunately freed ourselves from the idea that the gods and goddesses are involved intimately with the human condition. This hard-won freedom now separates us from the mythic roots that bind communities together and connect humankind to some transhuman resource. It is imperative that we re-examine our mythologies of psychology and religion from the perspective of the interactive possibilities of divine-human relatedness.

The heroic archetypes will be brought into balance through the realization that warriorship is only one step in the realm of mythic possibilities. The hero, male or female, always serves a queen/king and the queen or king, in turn, always serves a god or goddess. We have forgotten entirely this last step and, in fact, are weak on the first one. Two often the hero and the king are self-serving at the expense of the community.

A MYTHIC WARNING

Long ago we lost the sacred heart and we forgot the need to participate in the spring rituals of seed planting or the ceremonies that bring the rain. Materialism is now the basis of our rituals and ceremonies. We live the mythology of green currency and the free market. Money has become the symbol of the conquering king. Nonetheless, for many people today the accumulation of greenbacks is no longer a meaningful progression through life, and the myth of consumerism, whether the goods be material or spiritual, has fallen short. We have become like "The Young Man Who Would Have His Eyes Opened."

> Once upon a time there was a young man who
> was never satisfied. After he had learned the lan-
> guage of the birds and beasts he realized that there
> was much yet to uncover in the dark of night.[6]

How many of us are like this boy who can never be satisfied? No matter what we have, or what we learn, we are
always searching for more. The story goes on to tell us:

> Now this young man spent all of his time looking
> for someone who would open his eyes to the dark
> of night. At last he reached an old magician called
> Mana, who could tell him all that he wanted to
> know. The old man warned the boy in this way:
> "My son, do not follow after empty knowledge,
> which will not bring you happiness, but rather
> evil. Much is hidden from the eyes of men,
> because did they know everything their hearts
> would no longer be at peace. Knowledge kills joy,
> therefore think well what you are doing, or some
> day you will repent. But if you will not take my
> advice, then truly I can show you the secrets of the
> night. Only you will need more than a man's
> courage to bear the sight."

Of course we know that the boy, just like ourselves, thought
he had the courage greater than any man and he began to
learn of the dark mysteries from the magician. Did he even
hear the warning that there is a knowledge that kills joy?
Do we? We readily risk what we have for the unending
desire for more. Because we are not happy with the ability
to be in the life we have, the story goes on.

---

[6]The story here, and on the following pages, is from Andrew Lang, ed., "The
Young Man Who Would Have His Eyes Opened," in *The Violet Fairy Book* (New
York: Dover, 1966), p. 294ff.

The magician explains to the boy that to acquire the desired knowledge he will have to attend the banquet of the serpent-king and dip a piece of bread into the golden bowl filled with goat's milk that would be on the table before the king. That very night the boy went to the place of the serpent-house and what he saw was creepier than creepy and surpassed all that he had ever dreamt of. Thousands of snakes, big and little and of every colour, were gathered together in one great cluster round a huge serpent, whose body was as thick as a beam, and which had on its head a golden crown. The boy was terrified, but upon seeing the golden bowl he knew it was his chance to see into the night. He crept forward and before his fear could stop him he dashed to the table, took a piece of bread, dipped it into the milk and ate it. He then ran as fast as he could until he fell in exhaustion miles away from the feast.

Upon hearing this story, most of us would be pulled by the challenge of the task and identify the curious boy's actions as those of the highly valued hero's journey. After all, hasn't our young man overcome the powers of great mystery? Don't we all desire such accomplishments? How willingly we push ourselves beyond the limits of our own fears and think of it as heroic! But dare there be another possibility?

The next day our young man awakes surprised to find that he is still alive. After the fatigues and terrors of the night he lay still till mid-day, but he made up his mind that he would go into the forest that very evening to see what the goats' milk could really do for him. Once in the forest he saw what no mortal eyes had ever seen before. Beneath the trees were golden pavilions, with flags of silver all brightly lighted up. He was still wondering why the pavilions were there, when a noise was heard among the trees, as if the wind had suddenly come up, and on all sides beautiful maidens stepped from the trees into the bright light of the moon. These were the wood-nymphs, daughters of the earth-mother, who came every night to hold their dances in the forest. Eventually a silvery veil seemed to be drawn over the ladies and they vanished from sight.

As we identify with the heroic young man, we believe he has been rewarded for the hard task of stealing from the serpent king. We relish the idea of another happy ending. Is this not the Western way of hard work and just rewards? But the story does not end here; there is a surprise that offers another mythic theme for us to ponder.

The young man felt the day to be endless and counted the minutes till night would come and he might return to the forest. But when at last he got there he found neither pavilions nor nymphs. Although he went back many nights he never saw them again. Still, he thought about them night and day, and ceased to care about anything else in the world, and was sick to the end of his life with longing for that beautiful vision. And that was the way he learned that the wizard had spoken truly when he said, "Blindness is man's highest good."

What a shock to find that the heroic deed has led only to a longing that cannot be satisfied. How do we cope with a myth that suggests that there are limits to insight? Can we stand the idea that the dance ground of the wood-nymphs is sacred territory, meant to be hidden from human observation, and that the Goddesses have their own ways? This story challenges us to face the possibility that the sacred contains mysteries that are not ours to enter. Maybe the mystery, itself, is the bridge to transhuman realities. Pushing through mystery, as did this young man, can mean a life of emptiness. Living our "highest good" apparently includes recovering regard and respect for the mystery of mystery.

In an age where scientific investigation has become the model by which we approach all questions, whether social, political, environmental, or religious, it is difficult for us to accept that not everything should be revealed. It is painfully difficult for us to grasp the treasures of limitation. How angry we are when our bodies become ill and cause us to change our plans. Physical limitations are difficult enough; what about spiritual limitations? We who consider progress our most important product, we who see frontiers as something to be conquered, have a long way to go before we will be able to acknowledge that there are things better left in the dark and that there are mysteries that are not ours to uncover.

The "Hero's Journey" is the dominant mythology of the Western personality, and we cannot turn back what we have already developed, but we can question that journey. Today, as in no other time in history, we have choices about which myths we participate in to best contribute to the ongoingness of the grand mystery of creation. We can open ourselves to less known mythic teachings, as well as restore the integrity of those we have too readily dismantled. We can follow mythological guidance and reestablish sacred relationships with all of existence. Without a deepened sense of the sacred, we may become a society unable to be satisfied with life as it surrounds us, like our "boy" who wouldn't be satisfied with the language of the birds and beasts. The wizard warned of the dangers of this choice, but the boy of the story refused to listen. We may refuse to listen, too.

Today, even if we can listen, we often lack the relationship with the warning wizard. Although prophetic voices surround us, we refuse to validate their cries. As a culture, we have few shamans, elders, ancients, masters, priests, or priestesses who have the authority of spiritual and communal guides. We are forced to turn within ourselves and do our best to apply modern interpretations of ancient myths to our personal development. And while this is a worthy project that enlivens the mythic dimension, it generally falls short of deep sacred connection because we have only our own ego analysis to guide us. The depths of the human psyche can be the connection to mythic illuminations when the heroic ego steps aside; allowing the voices and the images of the unknown world to emerge.

Application of mythic themes to personal development is an important step toward health in a generally unhealthy world. But we must go the next mile. When Parsifal reaches the castle of the Fisher King the second time and asks, "Whom does the Grail serve?" his journey is not over: he must now begin a new life in service—no longer to his king—but to his God. Like Parsifal, we must move beyond the myth of the individual hero and reconnect to the ancient wisdom that leads to a greater than personal view. Unfortunately, Parsifal's story stops here and we will have to find our way without his warrior-king model.[7]

Parsifal reaches the Grail after having been taken by religious pilgrims to a hermitage in the woods. There an old hermit confronted him with his many mistakes, and at the same time told him that he was forgiven for his wrong actions. The hermit instructed Parsifal on how to reach the Grail Castle and assured him that he would find his way to the Grail and do his part in healing the kingdom. By the end of this journey, the heroic position is

---

[7]Robert A. Johnson, *He* (New York: Harper & Row, 1974).

committed to the right question and the willingness to hear the answer.

The Arthurian myths point us toward another, less traveled, journey: the journey of the soul in its ongoing relationship and participation with the divine. The connection to the transhuman and the invisible world are available, but the "how to" of such a journey has been sacrificed to the gods of rationalism, materialism, individualism, and the many other "isms" of our present world.

Modern seekers need to speak this mythic language again, to rediscover the stories that teach us about development of heart and soul. As we work with the bits and pieces that are rediscovered, we can enliven ourselves and our world. In the Hassidic tradition, our situation looks something like this:

> When the Baal Shem had a difficult task before him, he would go to a certain place in the woods, light a fire and meditate in prayer—and what he had set out to perform was done. When a generation later the Maggid of Meseritz was faced with the same task he would go to the same place in the woods and say: We can no longer light the fire, but we can still speak the prayers—and what he wanted done became reality. Again a generation later Rabbi Moshe Leib of Sassov had to perform this task. And he too went into the woods and said: We can no longer light a fire, nor do we know the secret meditations belonging to the prayer, but we do know the place in the woods to which it all belongs—and that must be sufficient; and sufficient it was. But when another generation had passed and Rabbi Israel of Rishin was called upon to perform the task, he sat down on his golden chair in his castle and said: We cannot light the fire, we cannot speak the prayers, we do not know the place, but we can tell the story of how it was

done. And, the story which he told had the same effect as the actions of the other three.[8]

So, the stories themselves must be enough. Stories are, in essence, the voices of our ancestors. They are our mythic connection to the unfolding mystery of life. Stories reveal the individual/collective relationship, the interdependence and interrelationship of life, and the quality of oneness or wholeness that includes all of reality, visible and invisible. The idea that telling stories and remythologizing the world in which we live can reconnect us to the divine mystery of life may seem too large a stance to take. Nonetheless, I risk it. The purpose and function of myth itself is to connect us to this greater picture and to guide us in our participation in its mystery. The power of the myth is its uncanny ability to turn life into wonder and daily existence into sacred partnership.

EXERCISE 3

REMEMBERING MYTHS

One of the ways we can get in touch with myth is to think back to the stories that we remember from childhood. What books did you read? What movies did you see?

1. Make a list of stories you remember.

2. Go to the library and find original versions of these stories and read them.

3. Be delighted and surprised at what comes back to you.

4. Reflect on the lessons of life that may have come to you through myth and fairy tales.

---

[8]Gershom G. Scholem, *Major Trends in Jewish Mysticism* (New York: Schocken Books, 1954), pp. 349–350.

Maybe you remember the lesson of "The Fir Tree" who needed to be happy where he was planted. Possibly it was "Little Tiny" who taught you about the magic of the fairies that lived in each flower? Maybe "Jonah and the Whale" taught you that God wanted you to do what God wanted you to do; or "Raven" taught you that life is full of funny tricks that end up bringing new ways of seeing. Maybe it was "Henny Penny" who originally gave you the idea that perception was all a matter of where you were standing. Beneath us all the stories perform their magic. Ideas we think our own have their background in the world of our stories.

CHAPTER TWO

OTHER HEROES

In examining the motif of the hero, it is important to focus on a variety of models, rather than assuming that we already know everything there is to know about heroics. Socially and psychologically the thematic journey of the hero tends to correspond with the beginning stages of adult development. The acquisition of a sense of self, a sense of one's power, begins in early adolescence and extends into the middle life years of 40–50. The hero is seen on the basketball court and in the boardroom. The hero gets a law degree, raises children, runs a household. The hero is not gender limited; women are every bit as heroic as men. The heroine is clearly not the female equivalent of the hero. There are a million ways to be a hero that are left unexplored because we too often equate the hero with competition, warriorship and "power over."

We have limited the hero by our modern attitudes. The hero does not have to be confined to behaviors that reflect only our drive for power and our spirit of competition. We can remythologize the hero by learning other stories that model different possibilities for heroic development. For example, in R. MacDonald Alden's story of "The Knights of the Silver Shield," we discover a hero who neither fights a battle nor conquers an enemy.[1] The heroic task for the knight of this story involves fighting his own desires and overcoming his warrior expectations.

---

[1]For the full story, see R. MacDonald Alden, "The Knights of the Silver Shield," in *Why the Chimes Rang and Other Stories* (New York: Bobbs-Merrill Co., 1924) pp. 10–22.

In the beginning of the story we learn that the sign of the most highly developed knight is a golden star that magically appears at the center of that knight's silver shield. When a knight has accomplished enough worthy deeds and won enough mighty battles, it is the star that announces that a true hero is among the people. Alden tells a story about a young knight, named Sir Roland, who hopes to become a great hero and win his star. The tale begins when the kingdom is attacked by cruel giants from the forest. The aspiring young hero wishes to be placed in the most dangerous battle, that he might prove himself worthy of his star.

As Sir Roland prepares for the upcoming battle, he is deeply disappointed to learn that the lord of the castle has appointed him to stay behind to be the guardian of the castle gate. He is the knight that must remain at home while all the others ride off to war against the giants. The glories of war are not to be his on this particular day. He is the only knight to be left behind. Surely, all of his heroic ideals are shattered in this moment. He despairs that his opportunity to win his star has passed him by. The young knight stands alone at the castle gate, knowing that his companions will succeed where he will fail. In staying at the castle, Sir Roland feels that he will never have the chance to fulfill his desire to become a great knight.

This is how each of us must feel when we begin to realize that we may not achieve that heroic goal so central to our life. Somewhere, we each have that desire that our star might shine forth, and that all the world will see our worth. How disappointed we become when finding ourselves tending life's needs in ways that are most unglamorous and un-heroic. When we are not fulfilling the image of the hero, we easily fall into depression and despair. Each of us, like Sir Roland, yearns to be a hero, and this yearning often leads to deeds well done, but it can also blind us to the value of performing tasks that offer no opportunity of standing out, or looking like the "winner." We will have to overcome the secret drive for glory if we are to stand firm at the gate when those around us march off to win their stars.

Sir Roland's story goes on to tell us that, while the young knight stands watch at the castle gate, he is confronted three times with opportunities to leave his post and join the other knights on the battlefield. Like the story of Jesus in the wilderness, the knight must confront three temptations. He must bear the tension of learning what voice to follow. The instructions of the king? His personal drive to win his star? The voices of a collective that places rewards on warriorship? Sir Roland stands at the castle gate facing what comes to meet him.

The first temptation comes in the form of a wounded knight who offers to watch the gate while the young knight rides into battle. The second temptation is from an old woman who taunts the young knight, suggesting that he is weak in staying at the gate. And, the third temptation comes from an old man, in a long cloak, who would give the knight a magic sword to assure his success on the battlefield. Not ordinary success, but overwhelming success! With this sword, Sir Roland is offered the possibility of becoming the most powerful warrior in the kingdom.

Although the young knight desires, with all his heart, to win his star by entering the battle, he says "no" to each temptation. We must each ask ourselves if we could do the same? Feeling stuck in a territory where we see no chance of becoming a hero, could we turn away from situations that push us in the directions of our desires? Could we manage to turn away from that which we hold so dear? Could we stay with a task that seems less important? Sir Roland says "no" to his greatest desire: the desire to go to war, to fight the enemy, and to become a conquering hero. Given similar circumstances, could we do the same?

It appears that the qualities of discipline, and regard for the lord of the castle, are what keep Sir Roland at his post. In each situation, at the last moment, he remembers what his king has told him. His duty is to stay at the castle gate. No one is to be allowed to pass. It is this memory that enables the knight to hold fast to a position that he has not chosen. This seems a discipline that our world often lacks. We live in a time where systems change so rapidly that we have trouble finding "the lord of the castle" who might provide direction. This relationship of king and knight, student and teacher, disciple and master is no longer an integral part of our society.

The admirable quality of the knight in this story is his commitment to a higher authority; in this case the lord of the castle. Here the heroic task is to follow direction even though it appears to be moving in the opposite direction of one's personal desires. The knight's willingness to listen to his master enables him to avoid falling into the trap of his tempters. In the first temptation, when the wounded knight offers to stand at the castle gate, Sir Roland responds, "A knight belongs where his commander has put him." In the second temptation, the taunting of the old woman at the gate, Sir Roland replies, "It is neither you nor I that is commander here."[2] And in the third temptation, when he is offered the chance to be the greatest knight in the kingdom, Sir Roland says nothing, but takes action to close the gate, so that he won't be tempted further. He is aware that he could break the commandment of the lord of the castle if he stays open to that which is being offered.

Once the gate is closed, the deeper truth of those who have tried to persuade Sir Roland to leave the castle is revealed. Before the young knight's eyes, the old man turns into an immense and hideous giant. Apparently, each of those who have come to the gate have actually been the enemy trying to work their way into the castle. It was only Sir Roland's discipline of staying with the voice of his king that kept the castle from being taken over by the giants. The story of this young knight, standing still amidst the pressures of his own desires, provides a model for each of us.

---

[2]*Why the Chimes Rang and Other Stories*, pp. 15, 16.

This model reflects the deeper purpose of a discipline that releases us from power-driven self-will and personal expectation. This model reveals to us that the behavior of staying true to an authority greater than our own is behavior that is heroic. This model shows us that what we think is heroic, and what is actually needed, are not always the same. This model says that we don't always know the "best" way. In our age of "rugged individualism" we know more about doing things our own way than we do about following instruction and not taking action. We know a lot about "doing," but very little about "being."

The story does not end with the closing of the gate, but continues to an unexpected conclusion. At the end of the day, after all the warriors have won the battle against the giants, there is an evening of celebration. Suddenly, one of the older knights notices that Sir Roland's shield has begun to shine. All the knights turn to watch. In that moment a golden star begins to magically appear in the center of Sir Roland's shield. The shield shines out to establish the importance of the young knight's behavior. This golden star establishes that he who stayed behind to guard the castle gate is the greater hero.

Here we see the power of discrimination coming from something beyond our personal interpretations. The authority of the star germinates from some mysterious source that defies analysis and explanations. Interestingly enough, the only other shield in the kingdom that has a golden star belongs to the lord of the castle. This young knight, who never entered the battlefield, turns out to be the only knight who reflects the capacity to be king. The one who seemed most unlikely to be a great hero, turns out to be the only one to win the star.

In the story, the king has already proven his worth. It is known that the shields reflect clearly the character of the person who carries them. The lord of the castle sets the standard for those who seek to fulfill their heroic quest. The archetype of the king helps us to better grasp the guidance in this story.

We are reminded to examine the quality of the masters we serve. We are a people who believe in questioning authority. We trust our freedom of independent decision-making. To balance our overdeveloped sense of self-determination, we can acquire the capacity to follow the mystery of magic stars, and kings who dare to follow them. The hero of this story follows a voice and a guidance that is more powerful than his own. Although he longs to follow his idea of the hero's path, he releases his personal determination to align with one who already carries the golden star.

Like Parsifal in his search for the Holy Grail, the young knight of this story follows a mighty king. For Parsifal it was a long journey from King Arthur's fellowship of the Round Table to the Grail Castle. When he finally made it into the Grail Castle the second time, Parsifal had to ask, "Whom does the Grail serve?" Without this question he would not have been the hero of that particular tale. In asking this question, Parsifal realized that it was not Arthur whom Parsifal must follow, but God—as symbolized by the Grail. Parsifal's quest led him to understand that all life was in the service of God. Sir Roland learned that to serve a king who knows the mystery is to acquire one's star. Both knights found new relationship to the divine energy reflected in the Grail and the star.

The lord of the castle, like Arthur, is a king who points his knights toward the quest for the sacred. In these stories kings were often considered the representative of the divine on Earth. The forgotten meaning of a true leader is one who serves the sacred and mysterious dimensions of life. This is the deeper understanding placed in leadership throughout cultures around the world. Whether the title be king, queen, shaman, emperor, or master; the position was meant to carry relationship to the spiritual forces in the material world. We have become a world without leaders who follow divine guidance.

I hear students say that we have no "elders." I hear the same from people of their middle years. Where are the per-

sonalities who point us down the path of sacred development? The leaders that would train the hero in skills other
than warriorship? Are they around us and we do not see,
or seek, them? Or are they unable to be participants in our
overly stressed life-styles? Elders may not be apparent, yet
we must not use that as an excuse to neglect the discovery
of the star. The Gods and Goddesses are still available in
the modern world if we will work to develop the undeveloped qualities of listening, waiting, and following. There is
no quick fix, no easy way into the mysterious world of
sacred living. Clearly, it will be a heroic accomplishment.
Kings and stars have led us into new possibilities before.
The pattern of the archetypal guide can once more be acti-
vated within the souls of each of us, if we make that
choice.

In Christian mythology three kings follow a star to find
the Christ Child. We, too, can learn to follow the star; to
rediscover the Holy. But, like the three wise men of the birth
story, we must be cautious. We must remember that there is
also a fourth King, one named Herod, who seeks the Holy
Child for purposes of destruction and personal power. We
must be careful to whom we give allegiance; we must make
sure that the Lord's, or Lady's, shield has a golden star
shining at its center. In our modern world, where possible
charlatans represent themselves on every street corner, it is
best to search for teachers guided by a star of greater good.

The star is a symbol for the divine light, the heavenly
wisdom, the holy possibility. When we follow a lesser commander we place our loyalties in graven images and false
gods. Like Sir Roland, we must acquire the needed discipline of staying behind and holding to our task. The opposite of what we want is often that which leads us toward
our star. In giving up our heroic definitions of how we
think things "should" be, we discover how things really
are.

In pursuit of the hero as more than warrior-king, I'd
like to look at one more story. This is a story where the

hero is female and where the task is, again, an overcoming of something in one's character. This is a story about the hero's triumph over fear. In the Polish folktale "The Crow" we learn about a "lovable" Princess who is willing to undergo great suffering for the sake of another's healing.

Once upon a time there were three princesses who were all three young and beautiful; but the youngest, although she was not fairer than the other two, was the most lovable of them all.

About half a mile from the palace in which they lived there stood a castle which was uninhabited and almost a ruin, but the garden which surrounded it was a mass of blooming flowers, and in this garden the youngest Princess used often to walk.

One day when she was pacing to and fro under the lime trees, a black crow hopped out of a rose bush in front of her. The poor beast was all torn and bleeding, and the kind little Princess was quite unhappy about it. When the crow saw this it turned to her and said:

"I am not really a black crow, but an enchanted prince, who has been doomed to spend his youth in misery. If you only liked, Princess, you could save me. But you would have to say good-bye to all your own people and come and be my constant companion in this ruined castle. There is one habitable room in it, in which there is a golden bed; there you will have to live all by yourself, and don't forget that whatever you may see or hear in the night you must not scream out, for if you give as much as a single cry my sufferings will be doubled."

The good-natured princess at once left her home and her family and hurried to the ruined castle, and took possession of the room with the golden bed.[3]

The fact that our hero is a princess who is "most lovable" tells us that we are looking at the behavior of one who is already royal. This is not a knight who has yet to earn his star but a child of the royal family, a child willing to give up all that she has in order to heal the sufferings of another. The heroic redefined as one who enables healing is a paradigm worthy of consideration.

> When night approached she lay down, but though she shut her eyes tight sleep would not come. At midnight she heard to her great horror someone coming along the passage, and in a minute her door was flung wide open and a troop of strange beings entered the room. They at once proceeded to light a fire in the huge fireplace; then they placed a great cauldron of boiling water on it. When they had done this, they approached the bed on which the trembling girl lay, and, screaming and yelling all the time, they dragged her towards the cauldron. She nearly died with fright, but she never uttered a sound. Then of a sudden the cock crew, and all the evil spirits vanished.
>
> At the same moment the crow appeared and hopped all round the room with joy. It thanked the Princess most heartily for her goodness, and said that its sufferings had already been greatly lessened.
>
> Now one of the Princess's elder sisters, who was very inquisitive, had found out about everything, and went to pay her youngest sister a visit

[3]Andrew Lang, ed., "The Crow," in *The Yellow Fairy Book* (New York: Dover, 1966), pp. 92ff.

in the ruined castle. She implored her so urgently to let her spend the night with her in the golden bed, that at last the good-natured little Princess consented. But at midnight, when the odd folk appeared, the elder sister screamed with terror, and from this time on the youngest Princess insisted always on keeping watch alone.

The elder sister illustrates the dangers of taking on an action out of curiosity rather than love. This sister who had "found out about everything" is inquisitive but unable to endure the demand of the hero's chosen obligation. How lonely the healing work turns out to be. Apparently few are able to serve the higher purpose of lessening suffering.

So she lived in solitude all through the daytime, and at night she would have been frightened, had she not been so brave; but every day the crow came and thanked her for her endurance, and assured her that his sufferings were far less than they had been.

And so two years passed away, when one day the crow came to the Princess and said: "In another year I shall be freed from the spell I am under at present, because then the seven years will be over. But before I can resume my natural form, and take possession of the belongings of my fore-fathers, you must go out into the world and take service as a maidservant."

This added request of the crow places another deed in front of the princess. Bravery, endurance and solitude were required for the completion of the first request. Now labor and humility are necessary.

The young Princess consented at once, and for a whole year she served as a maid; but in spite of her youth and beauty she was very badly treated, and suffered many things. One evening, when she was spinning flax, and had worked her little white hands weary, she heard a rustling beside her and a cry of joy. Then she saw a handsome youth standing beside her, who knelt down at her feet and kissed the little weary white hands.

"I am the Prince," he said, "who you in your goodness, when I was wandering about in the shape of a black crow, freed from the most awful torments. Come now to my castle with me, and let us live there happily together."

So they went to the castle where they had both endured so much. But when they reached it, it was difficult to believe that it was the same, for it had all been rebuilt and done up again. And there they lived for a hundred years, a hundred years of joy and happiness.

Joy and happiness for a hundred years are surely an ending that rewards the suffering and endurance of the hero-princess. We need to remember that the motivation behind this young woman's entrance into the terrors of the ruined castle was to reduce the suffering of the enchanted prince. She had no idea of any gain for herself. The willingness to take on suffering so that another being might be saved is the heroic model in this folktale.

In African mythology there is a similar story. A young woman named Mella goes to the cave of the Python Healer to get help for her dying father. When she reaches the cave, the serpent states:

"The bravest of your people have fled in terror from my door. Does such a small young girl as you are have no fear that I might strangle you and leave your bones about my cave?"

Figure 2. Mella overcomes her fear. For the sake of another's healing she learns to carry the great serpent. From Geoffrey Williams, *African Designs from Traditional Sources* (New York: Dover, 1971), pp. 72 and 105.

"It is not a lack of fear that I possess," replied Mella to the hissing voice that seemed to be without a body, "but a love and a caring that is louder than my fear, a love and a caring for my dying father who has done no wrong . . ."[4]

Mella carries the python, wrapped around her entire body, back to her father. The dying father is restored and Mella must again carry the serpent back to its cave. A relationship grows between the Python Healer and the young woman. Eventually Mella is appointed village leader and is honored for her honesty, her courage and her love.

Each hero receives his/her reward. Sir Roland acquires the star of wisdom; the lovable princess experiences joy; and Mella gains status in her community. These heroic figures were not obliged to participate in war or in establishing power over others. They were required to follow the demands of love. Sir Roland loves his king and follows his commands. The princess loves the crow and bears his suffering. Mella loves her father and promotes his healing. The heroic motivation in all three tales is something other than conquest, competition, power, material gain, dominance. These heroes are moved by the needs and requests of others.

As we look at ourselves in whatever heroic quest we have undertaken, it is important to examine our motivations. As the heroic ego grows within us, the desire to serve something more than our personal development is an essential step in growing up. Between adolescence and the mid-30s we are heroically forming ourselves and growing in self-definition. Motivations of self-image, achievement, acquisition, success, happiness, etc., establish the heroic goals. At some midpoint in life, our perspective begins to expand into the world around us. Our motivations fre-

---

[4]Merlin Stone, *Ancient Mirrors of Womanhood* (Boston: Beacon Press, 1979, 1990), p. 155.

quently shift to caretaking, serving the community, making a contribution or perhaps undergoing spiritual transformation. Turning the energy that was once focused on personal accomplishments towards participation in a larger context we begin to explore transpersonal levels of development.

EXERCISE 4

THE QUESTION OF MOTIVATION

The question of establishing motivation is important to the development of a mythic orientation. The spiritual practices of prayer and meditation are invaluable in providing direction for the ego. Solitude and learning to quiet the mind help to shift the heroic ego away from itself. A few things you can do to direct the ego toward a relationship to the transpersonal are:

1. Turn off the television, the radio, the stereo, the habitual stimulus of daily life.

2. Spend time each week being quietly by yourself.

3. Develop a rhythmic phrase that directs your motivation toward something beyond your present position and repeat it in your mind when you are out walking or involved in simple daily tasks. You could say, "My heart is filled with love." Or, "My desire is to extend toward the divine." A Christian could say, "Our God in Heaven and Earth." A Buddhist might say, "I take refuge in the Buddha." A Moslem would say, "Allah is the one God."

4. Learn to focus on your breath as a way of quieting your mind. Begin by following the steps suggested here.

A. Pick a place where you can sit quietly for five to fifteen minutes. This could be at home or in the park; at the office or somewhere out in nature. The only requirements are that you feel comfortable and that there is a sense that you won't be interrupted during this time. At home or in the office remember to turn off your telephone for those few minutes.

B. Sit comfortably and place your tongue softly against the roof of your mouth just behind your front teeth. To begin you may want to close your eyes to limit external stimulus. Later it may be helpful to practice with your eyes open to enable focused attention in a wider variety of circumstances. Slowly breathe in through your nose, allowing the breath to move deeply into your lungs. Don't strain. Let yourself relax while watching the breath slide slowly back out your nostrils. Breathing is a natural, physical activity. Meditation begins by focusing and paying attention to how breath moves through and around us.

C. As the breath moves in and out of your body let your mind pay attention by saying inside yourself, "Breathing in,"—"breathing out." These simple phrases keep the mind attentive. As you breathe "in" and "out" you will begin to find your own rhythm. Keep your mind focused on "breathing in" and "breathing out." As thoughts or emotions come into your awareness, allow them to float away like clouds in the sky. Each time you are distracted, bring your attention back to "breathing in" and "breathing out."

D. As you begin to experience the basic sensations of breathing in and out, you can begin to count the breath; letting your mind focus become "breathing in—one," "breathing out—one," "in—two," "out—two," etc., until you reach ten. Then begin again at "breathing in—one." Any time you find that you have lost count, simply return to "breathing in—one." Counting allows you to observe the activity of your own mind, and how it focuses and loses focus time and time again. Each time thoughts and emotions take over, the mind can be brought back to attention by counting the breath. There is no judgment about returning to "breathing in—one." It only reveals to us how focused or distracted we are at any given moment.

Attention to your breath is a practice that, once learned, can be used regularly in daily life. Times of feeling stressed or anxious can be transformed by basic breath work. The traffic may be getting to you on the way to work and a moment of focusing on your breath will help you discover another attitude within yourself. Practice is the only teacher. To develop your breath-focus further, you might try a class in meditation or yoga. It could also be helpful to look through the wide variety of related books available in your local libraries and bookstores. A good beginning book is *Taking the Path of Zen*, by Robert Aitken.[5] If your first explorations don't bring immediate results, keep looking and keep working with the breath focus. Be willing to take the time to find a centering practice that works for you.

---

[5]Robert Aitken, *Taking the Path of Zen* (San Francisco: North Point Press, 1982).

CHAPTER THREE

BEYOND
HEROICS

In archetypal psychology the hero's journey has served as the primary prototype for the process of individuation, but this model comes up short when it leads to individualism. The ideal of the "rugged individual" is part of the mythology of the American frontier; while Jung's concept of individuation involves growing into the specific persons we are meant to be. Words like becoming, germinating, maturing, living and organic best describe the process of individuation. In one of the *C. G. Jung Letters*, Dr. Jung says:

> It is perfectly true that I never described an "individuated person" for the simple reason that nobody would understand why I describe such a case, and most of my readers would be bored to tears.[1]

Jung goes on to say that only a poet could describe the "lordly beauty and the divine completeness of an individuated old oak-tree, or the unique grotesqueness of a cactus."[2] The emphasis is not on heroics, but on each living being becoming his or her own *entelechia*, and growing into that which we are "from the very beginning."[3] His brief description is as follows:

---

[1] G. Adler and A. Jaffe, eds., *C. G. Jung Letters*, Vol. 2, Bollingen Series XCV:2 (Princeton, NJ: Princeton University Press, 1975), p. 323.
[2] *C. G. Jung Letters*, Vol. 2, p. 323.
[3] *C. G. Jung Letters*, Vol. 2, p. 323.

> We will have no need to be exaggerated, hypocrit-
> ical, neurotic, or any other nuisance. We will be in
> modest harmony with nature. . . . No matter
> whether people think they are individuated or not,
> they are just what they are. . . . The criterion is con-
> sciousness.[4]

As one grows away from the monomyth of the hero, the
role of ego is to attempt to be conscious, to be awake. This
central aspect of personality—that has defined who we are
and how we function—must suffer a loss of power, possibly
even alienation, for the larger phenomena of psyche to
break into view. It may be time for us to move on, to say
farewell to the hero and to the warrior and to begin the
exploration of what lies beyond this archetype.

One of the ways that culture changes is through individual behaviors. To free society of warrior dominance
will be a long slow transition. Nonetheless, we need not
use that as an excuse for no change at all. Joseph Campbell's *Myths to Live By* includes his article titled "Mythologies of War and Peace."[5] In it, Campbell speaks of the two
opposing mythologies and how they are shared throughout the world's cultures. He presents asceticism, or re-
nunciation of the world, as the opposite of war, while
suggesting that there is a third mythological stance which
needs to be considered. It is a mythology that aspires to a
time when wars cease and there will be some kind of
"mutual advantage" in living with peace. Peace will have
to be reframed as something more than withdrawal, something that suggests relationships within a world of opposing forces. An image of peace might possibly be something
similar to what Jung suggests by "a modest harmony with
nature."[6]

---

[4]*C. G. Jung Letters*, Vol. 2, p. 324.
[5]Joseph Campbell, "Mythologies of War and Peace," in *Myths to Live By* (New
York: Bantam Books, 1988), p. 174.
[6]*C. G. Jung Letters*, Vol. 2, p. 323.

We each have some small part to play in the creation of new living myths. To stay forever heroic is to stay forever adolescent. Maintaining the heroic model as the ultimate developmental stage perpetuates a society of 25-year-olds who are avoiding the task of mid-life maturity. We, as a species, have yet to experience the actuality of a life lived in full relationship to the transhuman and nonhuman worlds of existence, visible and invisible.

Transformation of the ego involves the realization of a larger ordering to life. This awareness sets the dying of the heroic ego in motion. It leads to rebirth in relationship to the greater wholeness of life. Before we leave the hero behind, I'd like to include the story of "Sir Launcelot's Dream," a myth that begins to tell us about the transformation of the hero. Sir Launcelot once came upon an ancient ruined chapel where he decided to spend the night. He rode around the chapel but he couldn't find a door. Launcelot's inability to find the chapel door tells us of this particular hero's relationship to the sacred; apparently he has no access.

Unable to enter the chapel, Launcelot made himself a bed beneath the thornbushes and fell into a trance-like sleep. He sensed himself awake and asleep at the same time. It was as though the world around him had become a dreamscape. Launcelot heard voices in the distance and the sound of horses upon the road. The figures of a wounded knight and an esquire appeared before his sleeping eyes. The face of the knight was white as pure wax and the seeds of death were upon his brow. Launcelot watched as the knight and esquire moved slowly along the road. He heard the knight asking, repeatedly, if there was light ahead. At last, the esquire responded that light was coming from the chapel. Launcelot, too, began to see that the chapel windows seemed illuminated from within by a pale blue light, and the sound of chanting voices grew stronger as the intensity of the light increased. Launcelot, still half asleep and half awake, watched as the doors of the chapel opened and an ancient hermit, carrying a silver candlestick, moved toward the suffering knight. The color began to return to the ashen face of the knight and Launcelot was aware that this wounded one would be healed. The story goes on and we learn that

> suddenly the Holy Grail, covered in a fair white cloth, comes gliding on a pure moonbeam and rests near the candles—and their light seemed as dim as if the sun shone, and dim also was the light of the full moon in the glorious brightness of the Light within the covered Grail.[7]
>
> Then Sir Launcelot was aware that this was the Holy Grail of which he was in search, and he strove with all his might to arouse himself, but he could not do so. Then the tears burst out from his eyes and traced down his cheeks in streams, but still he could not arouse himself, but lay chained in that waking sleep.[8]

Although Launcelot is able to see the Holy Grail and witness its healing power, he cannot reach it. He is unable to fulfill his heroic quest. His own unconsciousness keeps him paralyzed. Staying forever in the heroic model could bring any of us to the same position: aware of the holy, but unable to make the next step. The story tells us that Launcelot's sins keep him from being awake in the holy territory. We, too, may have the sins of our lives keeping us asleep. Is this tale telling us that past mistakes prevent connecting to divine healing? Fortunately, the story does not end here. We learn later that when Sir Launcelot wakes from his dream, he rides sadly through the countryside

---

[7]Roger L. Green, "Launcelot at the Grail Chapel" from *King Arthur and His Knights of the Round Table* (London: Puffin Books, 1953), pp. 229–231.

[8]Howard Pyle, "Sir Launcelot Becometh a Recluse," from *The Story of the Grail and the Passing of Arthur* (New York: Charles Scribner's Sons, 1933), pp. 101ff.

until he comes to the place of the Hermit of the Forest. Here we find that:

> Launcelot laid aside his armor and he kneeled down before the Hermit of the Forest, and confessed all his sins to him. And the Hermit of the Forest gave him absolution for these sins, and he said, "Take peace, my son. For although thou shalt not behold the Grail in thy flesh, yet shall God forgive thee these sins of thine that lie so heavily upon thy soul."[9]

Our earlier question is answered. No, our sins do not keep us from healing. Forgiveness is available. The hermit brings an unexpected dimension of the divine to the story. It is the importance of forgiveness that Launcelot is not able to appreciate. As the story ends, we see Launcelot's limitation as he moves into the more remote recesses of the forest:

> There he dwelt in the caves and in the wilds, living upon berries and the fruits of the forest. And he dwelt there a long time until he felt assured that God had forgiven him. Then he returned to his kind again; but never after that day was he seen to smile.[10]

The ending of this story leaves cause for wonder. Why is it that Sir Launcelot is never seen to smile again? Is the loss of the heroic warrior so painful that although he experiences both forgiveness and the life of a silent soul-searcher there is no longer joy? Does this myth tell us that the only real life is the life of the sinless warrior, as seen in the wounded knight, and that it is only he that has the opportunity of healing? Is Sir Launcelot's life not healed? Unfortunately,

---

[9] Howard Pyle, "Sir Launcelot Becometh a Recluse."
[10] Howard Pyle, "Sir Launcelot Becometh a Recluse."

this is the general attitude of Western mythology. We have placed the heroic as our highest value and cast everything else into the role of second best. We do, in fact, expect to slay the dragon, win the prize, and live happily ever after. The life of the Hermit of the Forest, although it reveals the capacity of the divine, has not yet captured our imagination. Mistakenly, the hermit is seen as the loss of possessions, loss of relationship, even loss of life rather than simply the loss of ego.

We, like Sir Launcelot, want not only to define ourselves, we want to control the holy as well. The hero desires the sacred in the form of the Grail, the collective symbol. When the sacred appears in the dark woods in symbols more mysterious and unknown, we do not know how to celebrate. We cannot move to deeper soul until we can open ourselves to unexplored mythic themes and archetypal patterns. The sacred has an unknown multiplicity of forms. Expanding mythologies open the doors to greater possibilities of transpersonal relationship. We must not allow the hero to impede our way.

CHAPTER FOUR

SACRED MYTHOLOGY

The most neglected mythology of our day is the mythology of the sacred. While the hero dominates, the soul goes undeveloped. It is important to acknowledge that, psychologically, the hero's journey is the equivalent of the development of a healthy ego. As long as we think non-heroic mythology is empty of joy and celebration, as witnessed in the story of "Launcelot's Dream," we will surely miss the deeper possibilities of sacred mythology. The idea that religious development is dull and lifeless reveals our basic misinterpretation of the sacred. Divine relatedness includes not only joy and celebration but a union of oneself with the sacredness of life that leads to wholeness (holiness) of personality, and, more significantly, to awareness of the holy-wholeness of all existence.

The thrill in saying "I" am, want, need, will, eventually bows to the more mature position of serving life's "Thou." The strong and healthy "I" willingly lets go of heroics for a further development of soul. Midlife crisis could be thought of as an outcome of an unwillingness to grow up. As ego clings to hard-won heroic positions, soul life is being sacrificed. The most common danger at midlife is to substitute a role change for a soul change. Changing the externals—a new job, a new car, a new partner—will not meet the yearning of the soul to find its true expression.

The paradoxical nature of Jung's psychology, for those of us who follow his lead, is that after working diligently to find our true ego, we must next give ourselves over to the authority of sacred existence. Ego, or small self, is the center of personal consciousness, while the larger Self is the animating principle for both conscious and unconscious, inner and outer, visible and invisible.[1] Through connecting to Self we establish relatedness to the eternal within ourselves and within all life. The indefinable mystery of divine revelation, in its endless forms, is perceived in our consciousness through this deep Self. Our small ego-self makes daily choices for or against cooperation with this larger sacredness. Ego carries Self into daily living or leaves the sacred in the landscape of lonely memory.

In the figures of Mary Magdalene and Jesus we find an example of this divine relatedness. A woman, Mary of Magdala, is ill. A holy man, Jesus of Nazareth, comes to her village. Magdalene goes to this holy man in search of healing and ends up leaving family, friends, and community to become companion to the one she knows to be holy. We, like Magdalene, must know the need for healing, must turn to the holy dimension of life, must experience the holy touch upon us, and must stay connected to the truth of our experiences for the rest of our days. We may not need to leave the life we have, as did Magdalene, but we are required to follow sacred guidance.

In bringing focused consciousness to soul work we begin a new step in becoming more truly our own being. Like Magdalene, the experience of the holy changes us forever. Now, ego's job is to maintain relationship to the larger Self within the phenomenal world. Without the light of ego's attention, soul might once again be hidden in the activity of the archetypal psyche. Once "I" can endure a soul connection, experiences of the eternal interplay within the activities of an ordinary life.

---

[1] A common mistake in Jungian interpretation has been to limit Self to ideas of Judeo-Christian monotheism. In this text, Self is defined as the eternal, animating principle within all life.

EXERCISE 5

TURNING WITHIN

A soul connection is an inner development available to the person willing to take the time to turn within. The following exercise in image-making will help connect you to images of your deep Self.

To do the following exercise you will need a regular sheet of unlined paper, a pen, pencil, colored markers, or any other drawing materials you might have.

1. Draw a circle that fits the full size of your paper.

2. Sit quietly with your paper in front of you. Ask a question on this theme: What do I know of the eternal within me? What does soul feel like? Create an open-ended question that fits your way of asking about soul and sacredness.

3. Close your eyes. Focus on your breathing. Reflect on the question, not by looking for an answer, but by letting the question sit inside you. Begin by feeling soul in your body. Breathe and hold the question.

4. When you feel that you're ready and have some sense of response inside yourself, open your eyes and create an image in the circle. Don't think about it and don't make judgments about your image. Let whatever wants to flow out of your hands come onto the paper.

5. When your image feels complete, you may want to write down a few words that were in your mind while you were drawing.

Note: This exercise can be done daily to help you understand the complexity of the eternal within. The image, as well as its colors and tone, will change each time you do it, showing you that the deep Self can never be set in any final definition.

Sacred mythology is the language of the soul. As soul contemplates the unseen mysteries that lie outside ordinary reality, myths provide the roadmaps to guide us through unfamiliar territories. Mythic motifs can draw us into our own sacred processes of becoming. "Amor and Psyche" is one such myth, providing for us an exemplary model of the God-Human relationship. Each element of this myth illuminates the divine powers and their relationship to the human soul.

"Amor and Psyche" illustrates for us a complex, and sometimes difficult, process of waiting, listening, searching, and acting that leads ultimately to union with the sacred. As Mircea Eliade points out: "The road is arduous, fraught with perils, because it is, in fact, a rite of the passage from the profane to the sacred, from the ephemeral and illusory to reality and eternity, from death to life, from man to the divinity."[2]

This story reveals to us that wisdom and joy are born out of unification of the human soul with the greater powers of the universe. Unification, by definition, is the counterbalance to our present anthropocentric development. Unity demands relationship and acknowledges our human connection with the divine. Key to the secret of sacred relatedness is the soul's (Psyche's) willingness to search for the beloved (Amor) and to participate with the unfolding path that leads to fulfillment in divine union.[3]

Psyche is presented as a magnificently beautiful but unloved human being who has been sentenced to marry the God of Death. More often than not, this is the experience of our own souls. Not understanding the wonder of our indescribable selves, we limit our holy longings rather than risk the path of our becoming. It is not uncommon to silence the

---

[2]Mircea Eliade, *The Myth of the Eternal Return*, Bollingen Series XLVI (Princeton, NJ: Princeton University Press, 1954), p. 46.

[3]See also Madeline McMurray, "Amor and Psyche: A Deepening Communion," in *The Face of the Deep*, Gillian Scharff, ed., Advent/Christmas/Epiphany, Winter 1991–1992 (Berkeley: published by Gillian Scharff, 1991), pp. 16–20.

wonder of the sacred. The soul spark is left unattended; sur-rendering to a life of hidden divinity in the unspoken wilderness of our unknown selves.

At the command of the Goddess Aphrodite, Amor is sent to pierce Psyche with his love potion so that she will fall in love with the God of Death. Amor accidently pricks himself instead and immediately falls in love with Psyche. Amor takes Psyche into his own world where he loves and cares for her. The only restriction placed upon their rela-tionship is that Psyche cannot know the real identity of her lover. Psyche is actually held unknowingly in the arms of Amor, the God of Love. Surely, each of us knows such moments when an unknown "guardian angel" protects us from destruction. We sense its presence, its importance to our destiny, but our relationship to the holy presence remains unclear.

The unknown god keeps Psyche protected until the questioning voices (in this story, Psyche's sisters) prod her into bringing the Beloved out of the darkness. Here the myth calls us to divine awareness: eventually the sacred must be born and brought into the daylight. Comfortable as it may be in the dark luxury of the womb-like realm of mys-tery, the soul remains restricted without the face-to-face encounter with the god.

Following her sister's instructions to discover who her lover really is, Psyche shines a light on the sleeping god. He awakens and instantly leaves her. Although Psyche has "seen" Amor and lost him, she has acquired a conscious passion to secure their relationship, a passion she hadn't know before. The loss of an unconscious connection to the sacred holds within it the creative possibility of awakening a deeper and more living desire for the Holy Other. Psyche has lost her life to save it. Until now she was contained in an entranced coupling with Amor; but a contained and unexplored attachment to the sacred is not enough. There comes a time when each of us must thrust passionately toward deeper connectedness.

As Psyche seeks Amor, she is presented the four tasks that strengthen her and make her ready for the new unity with the divine. The human responsibility for reconciliation to the god is not accomplished in the heroic style of the ego, but in the cyclic manner of death and rebirth: each task contains a process of waiting for guidance and following the instructions provided. It is only her willingness to listen that will enable her next step. Each labor is a creation of cosmos out of chaos, birthing new relatedness to the divine. As Soul struggles to unearth the pathway through mystery, Psyche discovers an ordering principle that, when listened to, guides her recovery of the sacred. Seeds must be sorted, the Golden fleece must be gathered, the River Styx as the source of life must be touched, and beauty must be brought out of Hades. Initially, each task overwhelms Psyche. She is forced to face her own inadequacy. The one thing Psyche has in this journey is her unbound desire for Amor. Fortunately, this is the only thing required.

Each impossible demand is met by unexpected helpers from the unseen gods and goddesses. Psyche slowly learns to listen, to trust, and to follow that which is presented. The ants who sort the seeds, the talking reeds that know how to collect the golden fleece, Zeus' eagle (who can retrieve the water), and the wise tower that knows the way into and out of Hades, are all movements from the realm of the divine that lead Soul in her search to recover the holy marriage. Following the unfolding of this amazing journey, Psyche moves closer and closer to the divine. Slowly, profane existence turns into sacred reality.

The culmination of Psyche's pilgrimage comes when she must enter Hades to retrieve the beauty ointment for Aphrodite. Psyche is required by the goddess to move through the center of darkness in this yearning for her Beloved. Psyche's journey into Hades serves to warn each of us to not give up, to not let go in times of darkness, but to hold on and to remember that even in Hades guidance may be available. In the subterranean depths, soul is often kept on track by forces unknown and unseen.

In hopes of making herself more beautiful for Amor, Psyche opens the box brought back for Aphrodite. Because of this indiscretion, she is thrown into a death-like sleep, yet she does not die. At this moment, Amor, himself, intervenes on her behalf; in fact it is Psyche's pure motivation for the Beloved that saves her from her own mistakes and evokes the grace of divine intercession.

Here, the trickster comes into play. It is the "mistake" that calls Amor into action. Psyche wanted beauty, not for herself, but for Amor. The moment she opens the box meant for Aphrodite, Psyche commits the sin of pride, *hubris*. In comparing herself to the goddesses, she leaves herself open to forces beyond her control. The saving element, more powerful than her mistake, is that her intent was to please the god. We, too, will surely make mistakes on this journey toward sacred wholeness. There is no life that is without flaw. We can accept our mistakes if we remember that it is our motivation, more than our action, which determines the outcome. When our motives have been purified through devotion to the divine our mistakes often become our blessings.

The myth of Amor and Psyche provides a model of human development involving an enlargement of soul that includes interlinking oneself with the transhuman dimensions of reality. The intent of sacred mythology is to clarify the centrality of the sacred and to guide human development in its true purpose of coming to know the gods and goddesses. Like Psyche, we are held by the divine until we are called in some way to know more. When that time of differentiation presents itself, we pay the price by completing the tasks required of us. We learn to listen to the voices that will guide our deeper unfolding, and like Psyche, our love of the divine never wavers. The unyielding motivation of relationship to the sacred calls the holy other into response. The moments of our epiphanies, of our awareness of the holy, are by their very nature, gifts from the sacro-sanct reality called god or goddess. "Amor and Psyche" reveals to us divine unity—as both a gift given and a task accomplished. As the Soul moves toward the Divine, the Divine moves toward the Soul: human and transhuman intertwine in the sacred dance of ongoing creation.

The mythology of the soul's search for the beloved is what Jean Houston, in working with the same myth, calls a sacred psychology. Houston reminds us:

> In all the great spiritual and mystery traditions, the central theme, the guiding passion is the deep yearning for the Beloved of the soul. This yearning for union with the Beloved lies at the heart of sacred psychology, for it is this profound longing, which transcends the desire for romantic love, the nourishment of parental love, and all the multiple and marvelous varieties of human loving, that calls us to the Source.[4]

It may be helpful to turn to a Japanese story that is less lofty than the traditional style of the Greeks in their ever-strug-gling relationship between the human and divine realms. It concerns ordinary people, but nonetheless, it is about love and the divine. The title of this myth is "The Envious Neighbor."

> Long, long ago an old couple lived in a village, and, as they had no children to love and care for, they gave all their affection to a little dog. He was a pretty little creature, and instead of growing spoilt and disagreeable at not getting everything he wanted, as even children will do sometimes, the dog was grateful to them for their kindness,

---

[4]Jean Houston, *The Search for the Beloved* (Los Angeles: J. P. Tarcher, 1987), pp. 122–123.

and never left their side, whether they were in the house or out of it.

One day the old man was working in his garden, with his dog, as usual, close by. The morning was hot, and at last he put down his spade and wiped his wet forehead, noticing, as he did so, that the animal was snuffling and scratching at a spot a little way off. There was nothing very strange in this, as all dogs are fond of scratching, and he went on quietly with his digging, when the dog ran up to his master, barking loudly, and back again to the place where he had been scratching. This he did several times, till the old man wondered what could be the matter, and picking up the spade, followed where the dog led him. The dog was so delighted at his success that he jumped around, barking loudly, till the noise brought the old woman out of the house.

Curious to know if the dog had really found anything, the husband began to dig, and very soon the spade struck against something. He stooped down and pulled out a large box, filled quite full with shining gold pieces. The box was so heavy that the old woman had to help to carry it home, and you may guess what a supper the dog had that night! Now that he had made them rich, they gave him every day all that a dog likes best to eat, and the cushions on which he lay were fit for a prince.[5]

The old couple in this story reveal the process of soul-making. Like Psyche, they are fully human and fully in relationship with the Other that participates in their lives, in this

[5]This, and following material, is from Andrew Lang, "The Envious Neighbor," in *The Violet Fairy Book* (New York: Dover, 1966), pp. 160ff.

case the dog. This is obviously no ordinary dog, but is the helpful animal so often encountered in myths and fairy tales: the animal that knows where the treasure is, the animal that guides the soul in her task. The old man does the digging and together the couple retrieves the treasure, but it is only the dog that can reveal that which is hidden. The buried riches of the soul cannot be retrieved without the sacred helper. Like Psyche seeking Amor, a dependence upon the instinctual world is required if the tasks are to be completed. Most importantly, it is the love that the couple has for the dog that establishes their relationship. After the treasure comes into their lives the couple cares for the dog in an even more attentive way; the dog is now the "prince" in the story, the royal aspect that the soul-couple loves and tends. The focus remains with the dog, not the treasure. As the tale goes on:

> The story of the dog and his treasure soon became known, and a neighbor whose garden was next to the old people's grew so envious of their good luck that he could neither eat nor sleep. As the dog had discovered a treasure once, this foolish man thought he must be able to discover one always, and begged the old couple to lend him their pet for a little while, so that he might be made rich also.
>
> "How can you ask such a thing?" answered the old man indignantly. "You know how much we love him, and that he is never out of our sight for five minutes."
>
> But the envious neighbor would not heed his words, and came daily with the same request, till at last the old people, who could not bear to say no to anyone, promised to lend the dog, just for a night or two. No sooner did the man get hold of the dog than he turned him into the garden, but

> the dog did nothing but race about, and the man
> was forced to wait with what patience he could.

The soul-couple are unwilling to lend the dog, not because they don't want the neighbor to have a treasure, but because they love the dog so very much that they can never be without him for "more than five minutes." They have made the relationship to the divine dog central to their daily lives. According to the story it is the soul's inability "to say no to anyone" that finally leads to the granting of the neighbor's request. A generosity of spirit unveils itself in this country couple's willingness to share the dog with the neighbor. Possibly this generosity comes from the soul's awareness of the importance of the sacred dog to all of life. If our neighbor desires relationship to the divine—who are we to say no? Is not the dog meant to be shared?

On the other hand, the neighbor provides another caricature of the divine human relationship. It can sometimes be a relationship motivated by envy and the desire for satisfying outcomes rather than by love.

> The next morning the neighbor opened the house door, and the dog bounded joyfully into the garden, and, running up to the foot of a tree, began to scratch wildly. The man called loudly to his wife to bring a spade, and followed the dog, as he longed to catch the first glimpse of the expected treasure. But when he had dug up the ground, what did he find? Why, nothing but a parcel of old bones, which smelt so badly that he could not stay there a moment longer. And his heart was filled with rage against the dog who had played him this trick, and he seized a pickaxe and killed it on the spot, before he knew what he was doing. When he remembered that he would have to go with his story to the old man and his wife he was rather

frightened, but there was nothing to be gained by putting it off, so he pulled a very long face and went to his neighbor's garden.

"Your dog," said he, pretending to weep, "has suddenly fallen down dead, though I took every care of him, and gave him everything he could wish for. And I thought I had better come straight and tell you."

The shocking part of the myth is the power of the neighbor's frustration. When he doesn't get what he wants from the dog, his anger strikes out to kill the sacred creature. Seeking the sacred for our own purposes, motivated by something other than love, we create destruction. Like the dog, the divine does not survive our rejection. At this point in the story the suffering goes to the soul-couple, not the neighbor, because they know the true value of the dog. Both struggle and sacrifice are involved in the journey of the soul and, again like Psyche, the soul-couple must endure the pain that the divine relationship inflicts.

Weeping bitterly, the old man went to fetch the body of his favorite, and brought it home and buried it under the fig tree where he had found the treasure. From morning till night he and his wife mourned over their loss, and nothing could comfort them. At length, one night when he was asleep, he dreamt that the dog appeared to him and told him to cut down the fig tree over his grave, and use its wood to make a mortar. But when the old man woke and thought of his dream he did not feel at all inclined to cut down the tree, which bore well every year, and consulted his wife about it. The woman did not hesitate a moment, and said that after what had happened before, the dog's advice must certainly be obeyed, so the tree was felled, and a beautiful mortar

made from it. And when the season came for the
rice crop to be gathered the mortar was taken
down from its shelf, and the grains placed in it for
pounding, when, lo and behold! in a twinkling of
an eye, they all turned into gold pieces. At the
sight of all this gold the hearts of the old people
were glad, and once more they blessed their faith-
ful dog.

The relationship of the soul-couple to the sacred is changed
but not ended. The dog, once thought lost, reappears
through the dreamtime, giving instructions for human
behavior. The old man has little desire to do as the dog
instructs, but the old woman knows to follow the guidance
of the transpersonal. Again, the human must do the work,
cut the tree and make the mortar. When the task assigned
by the divine other is complete, the soul experiences transformation. Rice, the daily sustenance, transforms into the
sacred material of the sun. A new form of illumination is
now available to the soul in its ongoing relationship to the
sacred guide.

Of course, it wasn't long before this story also
came to the ears of their envious neighbor, and he
lost no time in going to the old people and asking
if they happened to have a mortar which they
could lend him. The old man did not at all like
parting with his precious treasure, but he never
could say no, so the neighbor went off with the
mortar under his arm.

The moment he got into his own house he
took a great handful of rice, and began to shell off
the husks, with the help of his wife. But, instead of
the gold pieces for which they looked, the rice
turned into berries with such a horrible smell that
they were obliged to run away, after smashing the
mortar in a rage and setting fire to the bits.

Once more we witness the misuse of the power of the divine, seeing that the outcomes are equal to the lack of sacred connection. The neighbor receives rot rather than riches. The soul-couple follow their original love for the holy as they have experienced it through their relatedness to the dog. The neighbor follows only his own envy and greed. A second time the soul-couple give over to the envious aspect simply because of not being able to say no, and again they suffer a loss. The story goes on to tell us that:

> The old people were naturally very much put out when they learned the fate of their mortar, and were not at all comforted by the explanations and excuses made by their neighbor. But that night the dog again appeared in a dream to his master, and told him that he must go and collect the ashes of the burnt mortar and bring them home. Then, when he heard that the Daimio, or great lord to whom this part of the country belonged, was expected at the capital, he was to carry the ashes to the high road, through which the procession would have to pass. And as soon as it was in sight he was to climb up all the cherry trees and sprinkle the ashes on them, and they would soon blossom as they had never blossomed before.
>
> This time the old man did not wait to consult his wife as to whether he was to do what his dog had told him, but directly he got up he went to his neighbor's house and collected the ashes of the burnt mortar. He put them carefully in a china vase, and carried it to the high road, sitting down on a seat till the Daimio should pass. . . . The old man had not been waiting very long before he saw a cloud of dust in the far distance, and knew that it must be the procession of the Daimio. On they came, every man dressed in his finest clothes, and the crowd that was lining the road bowed their

faces to the ground as they went by. Only the old
man did not bow himself, and the great lord saw
this, and bade one of his courtiers, in anger, go and
inquire why he had disobeyed the ancient customs. But before the messenger could reach him
the old man had climbed the nearest tree and scattered his ashes far and wide, and in an instant the
white flowers had flashed into life, and the heart
of the Daimio rejoiced, and he gave rich presents
to the old man . . .

A new level of development is seen in the soul-couple's
awareness. They have moved to a place of understanding
where they no longer question the dream world. The old
man knows immediately that he must complete the task
that the sacred animal presents. Relationship to the animating principle is firmly established, allowing the old man to
break the ancient customs and still find his way into the
heart of the Lord of the land. Soul development benefits
both the individual and the community. King and Kingdom
are enriched by the actions of one who follows the divine
revelation of the dream world. The Lord of the land is
touched and his heart rejoices. The dog is transformed into
a collective experience when the cherry trees bloom.

Our tale is not complete until we take one last look at
the envious neighbor.

We may be sure that in a very little while the envious neighbor had heard about the trees and the
old man's success, and his bosom was filled with
hate. He hastened to the place where he had
burned the mortar, collected a few of the ashes
which the old man had left behind, and took them
to the road, hoping that his luck might be as good
as the old man's, or perhaps even better. His heart
beat with pleasure when he caught the first
glimpses of the Daimio's train, and he held him-

self ready for the right moment. As the Daimio drew near he flung a great handful of ashes over the trees, but no buds or flowers followed the action: instead, the ashes were all blown back into the eyes of the Daimio and his warriors, till they cried out from pain. Then the prince ordered the evil-doer to be seized and bound and thrown into prison, where he was kept for many months. By the time he was set free everybody in his native village had found out his wickedness, and they would not let him live there any longer; and as he would not leave off his evil ways he soon went from bad to worse, and came to a miserable end.

The envious neighbor shows us the dangers of seeing the sacred possibility as an acquisition. By the end of the story envy and anger have turned to evil and hate. The soul of the neighbor comes to a miserable end while the soul that stays with love finds treasures, abundance, gold, beauty, and joy.

EXERCISE 6
───

MYTHIC EXPLORATION

In examining myth for psycho-spiritual development, it is important to remember that the ego is not present in the myth. Each element of the myth needs to be examined as a possible personality characteristic. In other words, your ego is not the dog, or the loving man and woman, or the envious neighbor. The dog, the loving man and woman, and the envious neighbor can be found in you. Like a dream, a myth can be an exploration of your deeper personality when you ask how each aspect of the myth reveals something of human behavior. Here are a few suggestions for how to use image-making and writing to explore a myth.

Note: These suggestions are developed around only two of the characters in the myth of "The Envious Neighbor." When working with a myth, it is best to work out all the characters to develop the maximum possibility of the meaning of the material. As with dreams, we tend to work with the figures we like best rather than with all the imagery.

1. Make a list of the characteristics of the envious neighbor.

2. Meditate on this character within you. Ask yourself how you have these characteristics. Be honest! Search your soul.

3. When you have a feeling for the character, use your clay or your colored pastels to create an image of this figure.

4. Now do the same three steps for the dog. Don't identify with one character over the other. Try to be an observer of these two sides of your personality.

5. When you begin to understand both qualities of human behavior, have a conversation between these two figures in your imagination. What do they have to say to one another? Write their dialogue in your journal.

Don't try to work out all the elements of a myth in one sitting. Give myth time to work on you as well as you working on the myth.

CHAPTER FIVE

INSCENDENCE

Assuming soul as expansive, flexible and ever-changing, then we hold within ourselves the possibility of psycho-spiritual evolution. For Psyche it was the love of something greater than the personal, the God, Amor, which led her to sacred relationship. In the tale of "The Envious Neighbor" it was the couple's love of the dog that enabled their following of invisible guidance, and it was Mary Magdalene's love for Jesus that changed her life. We, too, are capable of this love that connects to the sacred dimension of our lives. We probe the depths of our own souls to recover the lost myths of a love greater than human understanding.

We can explore mythology by asking about its purposes and functions. Myths can tell us about the structure of human behavior, about the structure of social order, about the structure of the divine, and from them we glean meaning that we may have previously discarded. Seeing into myth's purposes of connecting to the sacred and to community moves us toward the larger aspects of our humanity. Reverence permeates the human spirit as our relatedness to mythic consciousness grows.

In expanding the stories that surround us, we actually discover the stories within us. We all carry personal stories, as well as the myths and visions of our communities. We experience myths, dreams, and visions through the activity of the soul qualities (or what is called *Atman* in Hinduism) that are our particular expression of the divine. It is the task of the individual to bring the unseen powers of the archetypal world into attitudes and actions for everyday living. The structures of personality correspond with the structures of the material world. Most of us are familiar with the experience of thinking about someone and then running into that person on the street a few days later. We feel some sense of what we call "coincidence." In reflecting upon the concept of coincidence we can understand what Jung means by synchronicity. A simple definition for synchronicity could be "a meaningful coincidence." When we experience the coming together of an inner event—such as a thought, a feeling, or a dream—and an outer event—where thoughts, feelings, or dreams are experienced in the events of daily life—we are in the midst of synchronicity.

Synchronicity allows for the possibility that unknown forces affect our lives beyond our conscious awareness. This may be a new idea for those of us dominated by older scientific models. Accepting that there are forces influencing life that are outside human control is basic to both religious and mythic thinking. Stories of angels, coming to us from around the world, reveal the movement of non-human spirit forces. The highly developed mythologies of native people's relationship to the world of totems does the same thing. Angels and totems affirm the human as subject to unseen energies outside of our control, but within the scope of relatedness. In land-based traditions, the individual does not control the environment, but practices rituals that establish relationship with the surrounding world. The pre-modern hunting ritual, where the hunter calls upon the spirit of the animal, asking permission and thanking the animal for its sacrifice, is a clear example of an awareness that includes the connection between the structure of the individual psyche and the material world.

The significance of the deeper layers of the unconscious, of dreams, visions, penetrating insights, and religious experiences is not easily understood in the modern world because of our narrow mythic view. In the last few hundred years we have limited ourselves to an exclusive, rather than inclusive, outlook. The scientific attitude of limiting the variables for the sake of "pure" research encourages us to throw out anything that doesn't fit the design of the world as we want it.

A story told by James Willard Schultz in the book *Bear Chief's War Shirt* illustrates a way of perceiving, other than scientific, that is much neglected today.[1] In the mid 1700's the Blackfeet tribes numbered approximately 50,000 and covered the land from the Saskatchewan River south to the Yellowstone River. These people hunted buffalo by herding them off high cliffs into a huge corral, called a *piskan*, of dead and fallen trees, branches and brush. Above the corral, at the top of the cliff, they set up piles of stones in two ever-diverging lines for about a mile. The members of the tribe would hide behind the stone piles while one man, known as a buffalo caller, would act as a decoy to draw the herd into the pathway formed by the stones. As the buffalo moved down the path, the people would jump up and begin driving the herd forward until the leader plunged off the cliff, the others blindly following, into the piskan below.

This story is about a buffalo caller named Many-Tail-Feathers, who had been a decoyer for many winters. He was a man who had never failed in his work and in whom the people had great faith. One morning the members of the Pikuni tribe awoke to find that Many-Tail-Feathers had set their piskan on fire. The people were angry and upset until Many-Tail-Feathers stood before the tribal elders and told them of his vision. Many-Tail-Feathers told his people:

> My friends, my vision was very powerful. It was that I was walking in a valley strange to me when a buffalo bull came from a grove, stopped, and raised his right forefoot as though making the sign for peace. 'Peace! Peace!' I signed. Then we met, and he said: 'I have been looking for you. You and your kind are doing us a great wrong. With your

[1]James W. Schultz, *Bear Chief's War Shirt*, Wilbur Ward Betts, ed. (Missoula, MT: Mountain Press Publishing, 1984).

piskans you are rapidly killing off the buffalo. If you keep doing this, you will put an end to us. So this I say: Stop using your piskans if you would prevent a dread future for your tribe and all your kind.'

"What would it be, this dreadful happening?" he asked. 'I have warned you; I will say no more,' the bull answered, and turned away. With that, the man awoke. He was trembling, his body was wet with sweat. He felt that he must at once prove to his vision-buffalo that he had accepted the warning, accepted it not only for himself but for all his people. So was it that he hurried to the piskan and set it afire.

Said Lone Walker, the head chief, when the decoyer had finished: "Many-Tail-Feathers, you did right to burn the piskan. What our Sun-given visions tell us to do, so must we do if we are to survive the dangers that beset us."[2]

The people heard Many-Tail-Feathers' vision and embraced what he had learned. The entire community responded to one person's experience. The council listening to Many-Tail-Feathers decided that their people must never use the piskan again. They sent Many-Tail-Feathers to visit the Bloods and the Blackfeet to tell them his vision. In this way all three tribes of the Blackfeet Indian Confederacy ended the use of piskans. Tribal hunting practices were changed by one man's vision in a culture that still believed in visions. In these people we see the power of perceiving through a reality that the modern world calls irrational or superstitious. In pre-modern cultures, dreams and visions, speaking through responsible and respected members of the community, are the guides for survival and sustainable living.

---

[2]*Bear Chief's War Shirt*, p. 27.

For thousands of years, human beings have lived by animism, pantheism, sacred intuitions, and visions—practices that don't fit our contemporary models. For example, scholars of religious studies often exclude the practices of native peoples from the category of world religions. This narrow academic view is a clear reflection of limited insight into the archetypal world. We have yet to meet the challenge of expanding awareness into a world of diverse possibilities. One of the tasks of the post-modern world will be to give greater regard to receiving dreams and visions for the benefit of the community.

We must expand our mythology to fulfill its greater purpose of guiding us in understanding the invisible world behind the visible one. We can look both outside ourselves—at mythic material from around the world—and inside ourselves—for the unitive connection that is available within the structure of the deep Self.

Exploring the deeper layers of the unconscious establishes relatedness to the Self that is both center (inside us) and circumference (around us). Through working at soul-making we find the mythic dimension of our personal consciousness and connect to the realms of transpersonal existence. At the level of myth there is no separation between inner and outer, higher and lower, divine and human, sacred and profane, self and other. The mythic depths are our connective tissue to the rest of life. If alienation is our modern problem, then unity with the rest of creation is our solution. This is an easy statement to make, but it is a tremendous undertaking for a society that holds heroic power and conquest as its highest values.

To recreate a sense of our lost wholeness, the essence of most creation myths, we must explore the roads available to us—the stories and the human psyche—bringing what we discover into conscious living. I must emphasize "conscious" because it is easier to leave myth to roam in the territory of the unconscious than to manifest archetypal patterns in an ordinary life. For example, we love falling in love. This is one of the great mythic themes of western romanticism. The archetypes turn our lives upside-down under Aphrodite's influence. When romantic love loses its luster, as it always will, the ordinary relatedness of ongoing relationship is often sacrificed. Consciously making a relationship work is a slow struggle, more difficult than most of us are willing to endure.

The role of consciousness is to help us make the clearest decisions possible, whether concerning relationships or any other aspect of our lives. The belief that we cannot choose to help ourselves or change our society (deflation), or that our choices are always the best, not only for ourselves, but for everyone else (inflation) are egocentric levels of development. These attitudes of "no power" or "all power" lead to the same end: a position of separation from the whole. We become like Adam and Eve in the Garden of Eden. We are the innocent ones who help God in the work of creation—powerful—and the same innocent ones who blame the serpent for our behavior—powerless. The consequence of this mythology of innocence is four thousand years of patriarchal dominance guided by the duality between good and evil.

We each have the capacity to become responsible for the myths we're already living. We can say: "Yes, God, I did eat the apple and I do have the knowledge of good and evil." Until we, as individuals and as a society, accept responsibility for this wider range of knowledge available to us, we will remain split into endless camps of right and wrong. Our political candidates reflect how deeply this split is ingrained in our society. Campaigning for public office does not necessarily require that one upholds particular values or takes stands on specific issues. Winning a political campaign boils down to which candidate looks the cleanest and the most powerful. We want the good guy in the white hat even when we know he isn't real. When we insist on responsible answers to serious questions, the mythology of politics will begin to change. We will have to expand our ability to include both the positive and negative aspects of any given issue. Evolution toward a more inclusive mythology requires letting go of our presently one-sided approach to life.

EXERCISE 7

MEETING OUR OPPOSITES

We each have our own particular one-sided approach to life. Usually, our ego position is a reflection of this development. To expand our mythic perspective, the tool of affirmations can be put to use. Affirmations are used to make positive statements about ourselves and our life situation. At the mythic level, affirmations can be used to affirm the larger picture. Try working with one of the following affirming statements at the beginning of each day.

1. I will say "Yes" inside myself when I meet a person who is different from myself.

2. I will say "Yes" inside myself when someone expresses an opinion different from mine.

3. I will say "Yes" to something that I don't necessarily want to do today.

4. I will say "Yes" to life today, no matter what it brings.

Mythology is always on the move, forming the patterns of our lives while we slumber and turn in our sleep when choices nudge us. Myth is all around us: we touch it every day. We watch war on television as though it were a movie. We cheer for our side and raise our flags accordingly, without the slightest awareness that Ares, the God of War, is on the loose. We are stimulated without asking the deeper questions of what it means to send our young men and women to kill our newfound enemy. We have become desensitized to actual events through distance and technology. Life is presented to us in sound bites and television specials continually interrupted by advertisements. Eventually we think about the products rather than the events. "Shit happens," we say, and put ourselves back to sleep with games called "virtual reality" and "megagenesis."

If we do happen to wake up and take a look at the world around us, we don't seem to understand what's going on. We don't know from where the homeless emerged or why we are not able to educate the American public. We see no reason to protect the coastlines or endangered species if it means discomfort for human beings. When we look at the lack of fish populations, or the problems with the economy, we blame other nations and feel no sense of personal or collective responsibility. We act as though we are from another galaxy and have just arrived on planet Earth this morning.

Within each human being, the knowledge of how to be awake and how to walk the mythic path lies waiting to be rediscovered. In Buddhism the concept of enlightenment revolves around this ability to be awake: our ancestors in the pre-modern world also survived with wakefulness as their guide. Cultures around the globe have maintained contact with the powers of the mythic world as their path for living. The tribal people and cultures who have not lost this connection carry these depths into the world. Fortunately these cultures provide models that can help us recover our lost mythic connection. Concepts that outline this understanding of life include:

1. A belief in, or knowledge of, unseen powers;

2. A sense of mystery and reverence surrounding these powers;

3. Worship as commitment to the source of life;

4. Awareness that all life in the universe is connected and interdependent.[3]

These same principles are as applicable today as they have ever been. They are the common denominators of human survival. In Taoism we are taught:

> Without going outside, you may know the whole world.
> Without looking through the window,
> you may see the ways of heaven.
> The farther you go, the less you know.
>
> Thus the sage knows without traveling;
> He sees without looking;
> He works without doing.[4]

In Christianity we are challenged by the teaching that "the kingdom of God is within you" (sometimes translated "among you"). Kabir (as translated by Robert Bly) presents the same lesson:

> Friend, hope for the Guest while you are alive.
> Jump into experience while you are alive!
> Think . . . and think . . . while you are alive.
> What you call "salvation" belongs to the time
> before death.
>
> If you don't break your ropes while you're alive,
> do you think
> ghosts will do it after?

---

[3]Beck, Walters and Francisco, *The Sacred* (Flagstaff, AZ: Northland Publishing Co., 1990), p. 8.
[4]Number 47. From *Tao Te Ching*, by Lao Tsu, trans. Feng/English. Copyright © 1972 by Gia-Fu Feng and Jane English. Reprinted by permission of Alfred A. Knopf, Inc.

The idea that the soul will join with the ecstatic
just because the body is rotten—
that is all fantasy.
What is found now is found then.
If you find nothing now,
you will simply end up with an apartment in the
    City of Death.
If you make love with the divine now, in the next life
    you will have the face of satisfied desire.

So plunge into the truth, find out who the Teacher is,
    Believe in the Great Sound!

Kabir says this: When the Guest is being searched for,
    it is the intensity of the longing for the Guest
    that does all the work.
Look at me, and you will see a slave of that intensity.[5]

This archetypal pattern of the divine quality within the
human soul has emerged through thousands of years in a
variety of religious traditions. We have only to be touched
by this mythology of a living soul to begin to open ourselves to its development. Thomas Berry, in his book *The
Dreams of the Earth*,[6] talks about going below our cultural
coding to discover the "deeper spontaneities" of our genetic
coding. It seems reasonable to think of these deeper spontaneities as another reference to the archetypal psyche or
the mythic dimension. Berry helps us to understand that
these deeper layers are biological. The mythic dimension is
how we are put together; Jung called it an organic process.
This organic process is what enables land based cultures to
understand that they are part of a larger net of connections.

---

[5]From *The Kabir Book* by Robert Bly. Copyright © 1971, 1977 by Robert Bly.
Reprinted by permission of Beacon Press. See p. 24.
[6]Thomas Berry, *The Dreams of the Earth* (San Francisco: Sierra Club Books, 1988).

There is a biological experience available in myths and rituals. As Berry would point out—it is not the brain but the gene.

For centuries, Western people have turned to the transcendent aspect of the divine as the source of religious consciousness. Not only has "God" become singular and patriarchal over the last four thousand years, but He has established his residence somewhere off this planet. This distant deity has enabled us to neglect the now; "if you find nothing now, you will simply end up with an apartment in the City of Death." Our modern separation from "the Guest" leaves us without even the possibility of interaction with the divine creator. We lack creative possibility within our mythic structures and we know almost nothing about how to "make love with the divine now."

Not knowing our love for the sacred reflects the human condition of separation, alienation, and dualism. Seeking the mythic voice, we recognize the instinctive drives that give value to our existence. Berry calls this process of going into ourselves and our world to recover sacred connection "inscendence," the search for the divine through the descent into matter.

EXERCISE 8

WAKING DREAMS

One of the ways you can develop your relationship to the deeper spontaneities is to move into a half-dream state or what we call "day dreaming." This is easier to do upon first waking in the morning just before you get out of bed. Once you have established the ability to move in and out of the half-dream state you will find that you can do it at other times of the day as well.

1. Begin by staying quietly in bed when you first wake in the morning. Set your alarm an hour ahead if you don't naturally wake early.

2. Rather than getting up, let your body relax until you are nearly asleep again, but keep your awareness focused on what is going on in your imagination.

3. As the world of images presents itself; watch, remember, even interact with what comes into awareness.

4. As the images bring themselves to a conclusion, just as a dream does, get up slowly and write down your experience. The recorded material can be worked with later in art and writing.

In *Waking Dreams*, Mary Watkins tells us of the ancient practice of consciously experiencing images:

> Through the waking dream a journey was made possible. Either the gods or spirits were enabled to pass into our world, or we into theirs. The conjunction was envisioned not only as a bridge from one world to another, but as a plane of co-existence of the two worlds. Through the connection of the two, the individual was able to obtain gifts of wisdom and self-knowledge from the divine benefactors. One could learn of the spirit world. The connection of the two planes—spiritual and material—through participation in the half-dream state was considered to bring health.[7]

We can better understand the experiences of expansive human awareness through examining a few examples. The

---

[7]Mary Watkins, *Waking Dreams* (Dallas: Spring Publications, 1984), p. 15. Used by permission.

following four images are from clients who have, through dreams and active imagination, begun to listen to these deeper layers of their own being. In each example, an animal presented itself through the world of imagination, and was then developed as a helpful symbol through image-making.

In the first example, a woman in the early stages of therapy creates a drawing of a mythical winged beast that appears to her in a dream. In the dream, a fence keeps the beast locked in a green pasture; the wings suggest that this animal has the potential to transcend enclosure. The client knows almost nothing about this creature at the time of her dream; she is a bit fearful of something so unknown. As she draws her dream, she establishes relationship with the animal energy of her inner world, an energy that was fenced in and forgotten long ago. As she discovers this magical part of herself, she realizes that she has to release her animal nature from its limited space.

As she explores her body through dance, exercise, and massage, she comes to realize that much of her success in life came from her highly developed thinking mind and her ability to articulate ideas. Unfortunately, this development was often at the expense of her body. She is surprised to find that her body has ideas of its own and wants a different form of articulation. Mind and body have been separated by the fence of self-definition that views intellect as most valuable. This restriction of the body has also limited her emotions and her connection to the world of physical sensations. She begins to experience her presence in space and time. In turn, she realizes her influence upon given situations. For example, she can depend less on ideas about child rearing and focus more on the physical nature of the parental bond she has with her children. Through conscious attention to her own body she increases her choices in any given situation.

How many of us are just like this woman? We use our minds to override our bodies and sacrifice feelings and emotions to an overly intellectual approach to life. We think ourselves into positions that result in poorer choices for our growth. Intuitions, feelings, emotions, sensations, and images are often trampled beneath the intellect.

The magical creature of the drawing (figure 3), instructs this woman to enter more fully into her own bodily sensations and to listen to what they want. Our bodies are like the dog who encouraged the old man to dig up the treasure in the story of "The Envious Neighbor." The magical beast introduces a task to be completed if the treasure is to be recovered. The animal nature offers guidance for hidden wealth while the listener must do the work.

It is not uncommon to hear people say that they had a dream or premonition that clearly told them to do or not do something in a given situation. Most often, people dismiss such notions and go forward with exactly what they want to do. In hindsight, it is usually clear that the premonition would have been the better director. A man dreams that the

Figure 3. A mythical winged beast appears in a dreamscape. An unusual creature that encourages the discovery of hidden treasures within instinctual knowledge. Illustration used by permission.

woman with whom he is beginning a new relationship isn't available to him. Nonetheless, he goes forward in pursuit of her. Six months later all hell breaks loose and the dreamer falls into a deep depression over another failed relationship. Interestingly enough, he only sees the importance of the original dream after the relationship is over. How different all our lives might be if we could take seriously the messages presented to us. When we willingly include the unexplored parts of our lives, we have the opportunity of new discovery and, more importantly, new responses to life. Intuition and imagination are the neglected children of everyday life.

In a second image (figure 4, page 80), another magical animal offers expansion of self. A female "lion-dog" comes from a remote Kingdom high in the mountains to tell the dreamer about human relationship, about love. The dog's last words are: "I have wisdom." In this dream, a mysterious figure, almost other-worldly, emerges from the dream world to teach a higher knowledge. If this image is allowed to fall back into the world of unremembered dreamtime, an opportunity to gain wisdom remains outside personality in the territory of unlived insight.

Sometimes we remember the dream and interpret its meaning without uncovering a relationship to the image itself. Sometimes interpretation creates distance rather than connection. If I have a dream about a blond man who tells me that he is the masculine spokesperson for the psyche, I diminish his authority through naming him *animus*. If I have a written dialogue with this man, or paint a picture of him, I can relate to him as a living dimension of my personality. Relationship with this level of consciousness is more important than labels. It is through relationship that the searcher begins to grasp the wisdom that psyche offers. Images, like myths, have their own integrity. To follow the imaginal is to allow the mythic depths to establish a pathway for living.

Each dream, each image is a piece of our personal/collective mythology. By staying with the energy of an image and letting it have its own voice, we recover the deep wis-

Figure 4. Through the language of dreams, a female lion-dog speaks to issues of relationship, love, and wisdom. Illustration used by permission.

dom that comes from the objective psyche below our conscious desire to dominate life.

The third and fourth examples come from another client who began to draw images from her dreams and active imaginations when she reached a point in therapy where she felt stuck. The experience of expanding into image-making added a new dimension to her therapeutic work. As she participated with her imaginal world, she learned that the creative activity of making the images stimulated a shift in her awareness. She was able to move away from the focused consciousness of daily demands toward the more diffuse consciousness of connection to the imaginal realm. Working with oil pastels and paper, she released herself from the mood swings that had previously kept her mind spinning circles around the same problems without resolution. Her images allowed her to stay with the tension of an issue until it moved to completion.

While working with the material of the imaginal world, this client endured an ongoing restructuring of her ego as she learned to allow the archetypal energies of the psyche to guide her. As the ego gives over to soul-making, there is a movement away from the heroic position toward the affirmation of the soul's orientation to the deeper becoming. For this client, the transition from ego as dominant to soul as dominant came when images of the goddesses began to express "another world" making demands upon her personality.

As this woman reached a point of descending into the darker parts of herself, searching for the deeper spontaneities, she came upon a cave that had to be entered (see figure 5, page 82). Fears of the unknown blocked her entrance until images of a frog and a lotus guided her through. The feeling of this image was that there is stability within the fluid and ever changing nature of life. Again, the helpful guides emerge from the world of imagination.

Another image (figure 6, page 83) from this same client reveals the forces available within the imaginal realm when

Figure 5. Goddesses from another world watch over, and support, the soul's struggle for freedom. Through image-making the imaginal world is revealed. Illustration used by permission.

one is able to meet and participate with the archetypal psyche. This image is called "Star Woman" and originally came to the client through a dream. The dreamer awoke with a feeling of threat. She had not felt safe with a mother bear that appeared in her dream: the feeling was that a wrong move could bring trouble. The bear was watching the woman very closely. When, through an image-making process, the client took the dream further, she was able to transform the threatening animal into a helpmate.

It is important to note that the client did not have a specific outcome in mind when she began to work in imagination with the dream figures. When we recreate the dream world as closely as we can, and enter it without an ego-centered agenda, the imaginal world is able to speak its own language. To control the images, or to attempt to deter-

Figure 6. Star Woman is discovered as the dreamer expands her image. A place of nurturing activity brings relatedness to the deeper realms of consciousness. Illustration used by permission.

mine the task of the dream image, is simply another egoic way of trying to dominate the archetypal depths. If the dreamer had decided ahead of time that her imagination was going to work to make friends with the mother bear, she might have been more comfortable, but she would not necessarily have stayed in touch with the truth of the psyche. The animals of one's imaginal world are not always ready to be friendly; they may not want to help the ego personality. It is possible that one needs to learn to be afraid of some of the deeper parts of the psyche as a way of developing respect as part of an appropriate relationship to the animal powers.

In this case, the animal energy was ready to be in relationship with a feminine figure of the dream. The dreamer carried out an active imagination in which "Star Woman" fishes for food for the baby bear, while the mother bear becomes friendly with her. When the feminine aspect became active in the imaginal world, the feeling of threat diminished. As the nurturing activity of bringing food up from the depths continues, an old man appears. A figure who was not in the dream comes into the imaginal work. Although he remains silent, a feeling of well-being is added by his presence. The client experiences being inside a magical world that is alive and life-giving.

As we follow the world of dreams and images, it is not unusual for the ego to throw up roadblocks. Internal arguments tell us: "It was only a dream." "It was only my imagination." "These things don't really mean anything." These are all arguments that stabilize our old patterns. At these moments, a deeper knowledge, a non-ego position, must make the distinction as to what the ego can and cannot do. The ego's role is to do that which best supports psyche. "I" can nurture and protect soul-work by creating time and space to work on dreams, create images, write poetry or practice a religious discipline to name a few possibilities. In soul-work, ego slowly moves from a central position of power to a place of relatedness to the rest of the personality. Ego cannot remain the ruling principle if the wholeness of psyche is to be fulfilled. It is essential that "I" be related to the larger whole of creation to avoid the dangers of either inflation or disintegration. The larger Self described by both Jung's psychology and Zen Buddhism unifies the opposing forces within ourselves and within our world. What ego, or small self, judged, Self embraces. The powers of the mythic psyche can be overwhelming to the ego, while the Self is able to include even the most difficult possibilities.

When meeting the material of the archetypal psyche we need time to weave what is presented into the realities of our lives. We learn to contain the mythic depths of personality while not being identified with either the positive or negative aspects of what comes into consciousness. The awareness that soul-work is divine work keeps the ego in a position of seeker, student, beginner—a position of ongoing learner.

The five preceding examples give us a glimpse of the possibilities that lie just below the threshold of daily consciousness. We are challenged by these mythic processes and inspired to examine the images of the psyche for both personal and collective meaning. Every image of a dream or imagination is a message for the one to whom it has been given. This message must be worked with and brought into awareness. At the same time these messages are often much more than personal in their reference. A dream image is ours and not ours at the same time.

IMAGES FROM THE COLLECTIVE

As we grow more pluralistic our imagery becomes more complex. Renewed interest in Native American art and religion grows next to a developing school of Western Buddhism; we are interested in animism as it is being brought to the West, and mysticism from all traditions is increasingly acceptable. Sufi poetry and the writings of Thomas Merton stand on the same bookshelf. As our egoic stance of the hero moves toward transformation, there will be more and more weaving together of different traditions to create new and more beautiful patterns. The archetypes need new clothes for the 21st century.

In today's world there are still tribal cultures that have not lost their collective relatedness. It is to one of these that I turn to reflect upon the patterns of connection that still exist between ancient understandings and modern archetypal approaches.

Recently, British Broadcasting Company made a video of the last surviving pre-Columbian culture in South America. These people are the Kogi. The Kogi had a specific purpose in mind when they consented to be interviewed: to speak to the rest of the world through modern technology. It was an unusual decision for a group of people who have successfully lived outside the scientific/technological revolution. The Kogi have no electricity, no cars or tractors, no modern plumbing. Yet they want to communicate through the equipment available from BBC.[8]

When interviewed, the Kogi, who describe themselves as the "Elder Brothers," say that they have a message from "The Heart of the World"—the mountain upon which they live. They want to speak to those who live below the mountain, the "Younger Brothers," the rest of us. The Kogi have received a message from dreams, from rituals, and from nature, and they see it as their responsibility to transmit that message to us.

The Kogi have preserved the culture and spirituality of their ancestors, the ancient Tairona. They have carefully chosen their involvement with the world of the "Younger Brothers." They choose to use shovels and picks to make their labor more efficient, but they plant their crops ritualistically with planting sticks and see shoes as harmful because they break human contact with the earth.

For these pre-modern people, Earth is their creator and teacher. They call the Great Mother "Aluna," and describe her as the mind inside nature. The leaders of the community are trained in caves in the earth where, over many years, they learn the fundamental principles of the Great Mother. Through this deep connection to Earth, the Kogi have seen how she is changing and they know that something is wrong. At the top of the mountain upon which they live they experience that the clouds have changed and that the water is drying up. The Kogi believe that if this part of the mountain dies everything below it will die.

Because they know that they have not done anything to cause the land to change, they believe that they must talk

---

[8]Alan Ereira, producer. *From the Heart of the World: The Elder Brothers' Warning* (New York: Mystic Fire Video, 1991).

to the "Younger Brothers" about what is happening to the mountain. The Kogi want to tell us that we, the younger brothers, are destroying the world, and that we must stop this behavior before it is too late. They want us to know "that the world does not have to end. If we act well the world can go on."[9]

This is a straightforward message, one with which we are familiar. How did this premodern society, with almost no interface with "our" world, come to the same conclusions as modern environmentalists and biological scientists? Is this an example of the deeper spontaneities in action? Below the cultural coding of amazingly varied societies is the genetic coding basically the same? The Kogi understand that they are connected with the rest of us and that their survival is linked to ours. Do we understand this connection? Can we hear the message of the "Elder Brother"?

The archetype of the wisdom figure as expressed in the concept of the Elder Brother is one of the mythic themes that can help our global village find its holy center. Wisdom figures are found in many traditions. The teachers, the prophets, the shaman, and the sages are all figures who guide the collective toward healing and sacred living.

It may be helpful to expand the qualities of this particular wisdom figure for greater understanding of the mythic importance of the Kogi's decision to speak to us. In the Pima creation myths of North America there is a powerful ancestral figure known as Siuhu or as Elder Brother. Elder Brother lives in the mountains and watches over the people. He is both tribal protector and disciplinarian. The Elder Brother emerges from time to time to tend the people, but he always retreats back through a great maze to his mountain solitude. The Elder Brother is distant, mysterious and powerful. He emerges from the labyrinth only to help his people.

---

[9]See *From the Heart of the World: The Elder Brothers' Warning.*

As modern people dependent on the power of the individual, we are no longer familiar with guiding and protecting archetypes. We need to enliven our relationship to the transpersonal powers directed to the needs of the community. We need to accept the demand of the archetypal psyche, not only for our personal lives, but for what it asks of us for the sake of the collective. We must be as brave as the Kogi facing the unknown video cameras and speak the deep knowledge revealed to us. Until we awaken the deeper spontaneities within, our wisdom remains in the land of the sleeping giants.

CHAPTER SIX

MEETING
THE GIANTS

When we wrestle with the parts of our lives, whether personal or collective, that feel threatening, we need a mythology more inclusive than that of the patriarchal heavenly judge. In struggling against old mythologies of the godhead there is the tendency to discard the sacred altogether, or try to live mythologies that exclude darkness and difficulty. I often see people who have given up on the idea of God because they had believed that "He" was only good. When their lives didn't work out in the "good" ways that they had planned, there was no room for their innocent ideas of the divinity. Thus God had to be thrown out. Jung was critical of Christianity for just this reason. A God that is seen as only "good" leads to one-sided thinking in our religion, our philosophy, and in our general approach to life. If the future is to be an age capable of living with diversity, this Western one-sided propensity toward limiting the divine will have to be outgrown. Living mythologies of the sacred will need to be expansive enough to bear the tensions of light and dark, good and evil, successes and failures.

Today, mythology is being enlivened in what is commonly referred to as "New Age" thinking. Here, too, there is often too much emphasis on the light, perpetuating the old problem which needs to be transformed. Mythologies adequate to the demands of our present planetary situation will push for further development of our ideas and images of god, of society, and of individual behaviors. It is all too easy to use myth to support what we have and who we are, rather than to look for themes that challenge us to change. A common outlook of the New Age is that "everything is perfect just as it is." I can't help but think that the person telling me this is simply saying, "I like the life I have," or "I'm unwilling to challenge the status quo." Another popular philosophy is that "we create our own reality." I hear in this view someone who is saying either, "I like the life I have," or "I'll get the life I want." It is imperative that we not misuse mythologies of whole systems to support our position of comfort while avoiding that which is wrong within ourselves, within our society, within our world. For example, the Taoist teaching presented below may be misused as an excuse for not dealing with the negative aspects of our lives; rather than used appropriately to evoke a deeper awareness of the sacred movement of the universe.

> Do you think you can take over the universe and improve it?
> I do not believe it can be done.
>
> The universe is sacred.
> You cannot improve it.
> If you try to change it, you will ruin it.
> If you try to hold it, you will lose it.
> So sometimes things are ahead and sometimes they are behind;
> Sometimes breathing is hard, sometimes it comes easily;
> Sometimes there is strength and sometimes weakness;
> Sometimes one is up and sometimes down.
>
> Therefore the sage avoids extremes, excesses, and complacency.[1]

---

[1]Number 29. From *Tao Te Ching* by Lao Tsu, trans. Feng/English. Copyright © 1972 by Gia-Fu Feng and Jane English. Reprinted by permission of Alfred A. Knopf.

With insight into the sacred universe that cannot be improved, we would surely become like the sage whose behavior aligns with this sacred ordering principle. Unfortunately, we tend to avoid investigating what it would mean to live with a deepening understanding of how life works. Instead, we unconsciously misuse mythologies of wholeness to justify our extremes, excesses, and complacency. To embrace a mythology is to work to understand and live by it, not use it to absolve our behavior. Myths provide us with models for human behavior that are based on the conduct of the gods, the sages, and the masters.

Although the model of the heroic warrior-king is primary to Western mythology, it, too, needs expansion for the modern world. Psychologically, the heroic ego leads us on the journey of slaying the dragons that are the limitations of our lives. Each woman and man who knows the warrior part of herself or himself, and has integrated that energy into the personality, can function more fully in the everyday. For example, the person who has overcome the dragon of addiction, of depression, or of the fears that would block life, is heroic in this battle. Nonetheless, there comes a time when the battle ends—not necessarily because the problems are all gone, but because life's tasks need to be met in different ways.

As important as our heroic quest is, the time comes to leave the sword and shield behind. We will do this more readily if we know stories of gods and goddesses who function in other ways. Norse mythology provides an interesting framework for coming to know the giants rather than slaying them. Fighting is not always the answer.

According to the ancient mythology of the Norse tradition, creation consists of nine worlds. In the story that follows we will look at two of these worlds and their relationship to one another. These worlds are Asgard, the world of the gods, and Jotunheim, the world of the giants and trolls. The title of the story is *Odin, the All-Father*, and it is about Odin as he sits upon his throne in Asgard. From this throne, called the Lidskjalf, Odin can view all of Asgard and even into Jotunheim to see how the giants, or *jotuns*, are occupying themselves. Ordinarily, no other gods or goddesses are allowed to sit on Odin's throne, but sometimes he lets Frigg, his dearest wife, share it with him. So Odin and Frigg are capable of knowing all the secrets of the world.

Each day Odin sent two black ravens to fly over the world to see what they might bring back to him. Each evening Odin's ravens returned to him to whisper into his ear all the secret things they had learned. As Odin saw into the depths of Jotunheim, he knew that the wild jotuns hated men, as well as gods, and that they were always working toward destruction of the world.

But Odin saw one jotun named Mimir, who was wise and not wild. He was the owner of a magic spring that welled up where one of Yggdrasil's roots (the world tree) ended in Jotunheim. It was the Well of Wisdom. In it lay hidden all the knowledge of the age-old race of the jotuns, and Mimir, who quenched his thirst at the well each morning, was the wisest of the wise.

Odin went to Mimir and asked if he, too, might drink from his well. Mimir was too wise to hate the Aesir, but he would let him drink only if, in return, Odin would share his all-seeing sight. So Odin gave his left eye to Mimir and drank. After that Odin was the wisest of the wise, for he had the wisdom of both jotuns and Aesir. Of course, he was one-eyed now and so he always kept half of his face hidden by a wide-brimmed hat or a strand of his hair. But his remaining eye gleamed brighter than ever.

Mimir hid Odin's eye deep in the Well of Wisdom, and when he looked down through it, he

could see everything in the wide world. From then
on, he was Odin's great friend and adviser.[2]

Here we have a mythology where the gods and giants come
together. In fact, they make an exchange and become
friends and advisers. Because of Odin and Mimir, the two
worlds—one of gods and one of trolls—come together. This
same mythic theme is presented in Hebrew scripture in the
Book of Job, where Satan is an adviser to God, and in Taoism, when it teaches us to know the white, but keep the
black! In Hinduism, the figure of Shiva is both creator and
destroyer, erotic and ascetic, mild and mad. The mythology of unified opposites is an archetypal pattern found
throughout the world; it is a theme that pushes our psychological development to a new level. Heroics keep us slaying
the dragon. Becoming wise requires a new relationship to
that which has been known as enemy.

In the Norse story, the land of the giants and trolls
holds a level of wisdom that is not in the land of the gods.
This is a psychological reality as well as a mythic theme.
Within each of us there is some dark knowledge that, if valued, would guide us toward becoming more complete. We
need the sight of Odin to see into ourselves to acknowledge
that there is a lack within us and that we can learn from this
feared part of ourselves. We must also be willing to make
the required sacrifice to acquire wisdom.

Odin does not kill Mimir. He does not even engage
him in battle. He sees what Mimir has gained from relatedness to the root, the deep, dark underground part of the
world tree. Odin knows that his ability to see the whole
world is limited because he does not know what Mimir, his
shadow twin, knows. A great hero god gains wisdom
through relatedness to the world of the enemy. We must do
the same. Our worlds, within and around us, contain much

[2]Ingri D'Aulaire and Edgar P. D'Aulaire. *D'Aulaires' Norse Gods and Giants* (Garden City: Doubleday, 1967), pp. 38ff.

unfaced darkness and destructive possibility. To come to terms with these more difficult parts of ourselves and our environment, soul-work is required. Bringing the destructive and the creative together lies within the capacity of the human psyche. The Odin, Asgard world, and the Mimir, Jotunheim world meet at the deep root of soul.

The following waking dream illustrates the kind of darkness that must be faced as one lives related to the mythic deeps of these times.

A MYTH: WHAT'S IN IT FOR MOTHER EARTH?

Once upon a time there was a society living on Mother Earth whose people loved examining and analyzing information so much that they applied those skills to everything that they encountered. They called themselves "scientific" and took great pride in being part of the "Age of Information." Anything that could be measured and statistically verified automatically had great value. Leaders' qualities were judged on their ability to either analyze or manipulate information: the analysts were called "scholars" and those who used the information were called "politicians." Everyone else in the society was referred to as "the general populace." There were a few persons of unusual talent who could both analyze and use information. They, naturally, were the most powerful; they were called the "technocrats."

One of the beliefs basic to the Scientific Society was that people (well, not all people, but the people most like the leaders) are the most important species on Earth. There was general agreement that Earth had been created for the pleasure and well-being of mankind (again, meaning themselves).

Boiled down, this outlook meant, "What's in it for me?" Of course, this was stated more graciously. No one with any stature would openly ask, "What's in it for me?" Instead, they would say such and such was done for the welfare of the people, or for the security of the future. Reassurances like these comforted the general populace and all was well in the Scientific Society.

Certain scholars examined details within fields called biology and physics: the biologists investigated organic and inorganic properties of matter, while physicists scrutinized the properties and interactions of matter and energy. Some of the scholars in biology concluded that people were depleting the resources of the Earth; predicting that once these resources were gone, the general populace was going to be in serious trouble. Other scholars began to see that the energy within and surrounding Earth interfaced with human behavior; some said that many of these interactions were detrimental to both people and the planet.

This new information seemed to suggest that human beings were not totally self-sufficient, nor were they necessarily the center of the world. The politicians realized that looking at lost resources in this way caused the general populace discomfort, so they deemed the collected facts and figures "not in the best interests of the people." The leaders feared that if the general populace put any stock in these ideas they might decide that the technocrats had lost their ability to use information effectively; this was a chance the leaders would not take.

The leaders feared that such research could potentially undermine the ancient myths of the Scientific Society: the myths that told how the

Figure 7. The Fool embraces Mother Earth when the soul comes to know the interconnections and interrelationships that infuse the world. Illustration used by permission.

Earth had been divinely created for the pleasure of the original man, the one they called Adam. Over the centuries, this pleasing of Adam had been called many things. It had once been known as "The Enlightenment." Later, it was called "The New Frontier." At the time of this story, it was referred to as "The Scientific-Technological Revolution." Whatever the name given, the theme remained the same: everything discovered and developed was accommodated to the convenience of the people. The more powerful the people were, the more pleasure and gratification they felt they deserved.

It was clear that the revolutionary notion of resource depletion would have to be watchdogged to assure that the general populace would not be disturbed. Another method used to protect the people from this disturbing knowledge was to discredit anything that might cause alarm. The general populace, of course, was relieved to have bothersome data revealed as untrue. Simple communication systems, called the public press, carried out the job of reassuring the general populace that their comfort was secure. The following is a typical example of what was called a "press release":

A leak at the Indian Point nuclear power plant spilled more than 8,000 gallons of 'slightly radioactive' water into the Hudson River before it was detected Saturday, the plant's owner, Consolidated Edison said.

Spokesmen for the utility and the Nuclear Regulatory Commission said the leak posed no danger to the public or personnel at the plant in Buchanan, N.Y., about 30 miles north of New York City.

Storing, but not revealing, disturbing information enabled the scholars to go forward with their research. They could collect, measure, and examine matters while the general populace would be shielded from all things annoying.

Eventually, through scientific advance and a huge financial investment, science began transmitting information through space. One of the benefits of this was the ability to communicate beautiful pictures of Earth into the homes of the general populace; this had the effect of making them feel more than ever that the Earth was theirs. However, some scholars, who were labeled "the minority opinion" studied the pictures of Earth and dared to question the theory that it was simply an object created for the pleasure of people. When such scientists spoke out, they were labelled either "fools" or "trouble-makers" and were isolated to their own communities where they shared their ideas only among themselves.

At last, after some tumultuous years, the Scientific Society seemed to be running along smoothly. Perhaps our story would have ended here if it hadn't been for action taken by the Earth herself.

One day, the Earth seemed to realize her danger. Human creatures became more than she could bear; she knew that she must free herself of the wildly-multiplying cancer growing on her skin. At first, she began to shake, then rumble deep within. At her core, she vibrated, pulsated and generated an untapped energy source. Inside her glorious blue-green body, the fire flowed passionately through her veins. Volcanic fissures spewed forth molten red-hot lava and gray-grit ash. Earth became a fire-breathing dragon charging through space. Then, as abruptly as the spasm began, it stopped, and Earth stabilized herself. Now ravaged and scarred, her once life-filled skin felt the wounding pain, but at least she could relax now, knowing that, with most of the people and all but a few of the smaller life forms gone, she would eventually regenerate.

Later historians would suggest that the Earth had acted purposefully in her "great explosion." They also suggested that Earth's primary purpose had been to free herself of the human disease, but that her secondary purpose had been to teach people how to live in relationship to her whole system rather than by their own designs. To this day, there is speculation about why a few human creatures, most noticeably a large proportion of "fools" and "trouble-makers," lived. It may have been that Earth simply couldn't destroy them all; it may have been a sentimental attachment to people as a part of her living system.

Today, people wonder at the survival of their species. Was it purely random? Has Earth a purpose for this particular creature? These are the questions of our day. We search continually to understand the great mystery of our survival and our relationship to Earth. In this searching, we have learned that answers are to be found by going to her sacred mountains, sitting by her sacred streams and asking, "What's in it for Mother Earth?"[3]

The dreamer of this dream story was naturally shocked by such dark images. Nonetheless, there is an opportunity here to become like "Odin—The All Father" in seeing into the furthest reaches of many worlds. Environment plays an

---

[3]This dream provided by a patient. Used by permission.

enormous role in the formation of myth. People living in an
ice world know that the giants of ice and frost can be the
bringers of death. Survival requires consciousness of that
which threatens existence. Today's mythmakers spin stories
around the elements of our environment, requiring them to
speak of survival. The story presented here comes from the
imaginal world of a modern person looking into the
destructive forces of the 20th century.

To look into the face of the enemy, i.e., the one who
threatens destruction, is still a task for our time. Mythologies of embracing the enemy are solidly instilled in both
Eastern and Western traditions. The living of these ideals is
accomplished by only a few. Like the gods, the few set the
model for the many. In his autobiography, *Freedom In Exile*,
The Dalai Lama says:

> I took note of the Buddha's teaching that in one
> sense a supposed enemy is more valuable than a
> friend, for an enemy teaches you things, such as
> forbearance, that a friend generally does not.[4]

There is always something more to be learned. Often the
needed teachings come from one's enemy rather than one's
friends. We, like Odin, must see into the face of that which
we fear or see as enemy. In the turning toward fear we
recover the connection that is apparent between the "Warning of the Elder Brothers" from the ancient culture of the
Kogi and the modern North American Dreamer who asks;
"What's in it for Mother Earth?" These two voices, cultur-
ally so far apart, share the same mythological purposes—
survival and relationship of the human in the natural
world. These similar, but separate, experiences are the
mythology of evolution struggling to be included in modern consciousness.

---

[4]His Holiness The Dalai Lama, *Freedom in Exile: The Autobiography of the Dalai
Lama* (New York: HarperCollins, 1990), p. 81.

We poison the environment, as well as ourselves, while pretending otherwise. Our instinct for survival knows that this destructive behavior must be faced, integrated, and transformed. Some unacknowledged realm of consciousness knows that species survival can come through relationship to our destructive dragons. We will wrestle with the myths that can guide us toward a healthier future—myths that face darkness and its power for destruction and healing, myths that recover wisdom from its hidden wells, myths that make the sacrifice of the smaller view.

Chapter Seven

EMBRACING
THE SHADOW

We generally avoid the negative, stay away from people we don't like, and shun looking at our own flaws. Abusive families hide their destructive secrets, and abusive nations try to do the same. This may be a short-term psychological survival tool, but what survives is the abuse. We tend to adapt to the negative aspects of life rather than make changes. For example, a person working long and difficult hours usually receives body signals of stress. Through headaches, neckaches, pains in the chest or lower back, the body sends out its message to slow down. The willful mind controls or ignores physical sensations, interpreting illness as weakness, and giving status to living in the fast lane. Daily abuse of body and spirit are the result of ongoing negative behaviors.

Incorporating one's shadow qualities into personal consciousness is the task of each individual daring to seek wholeness. The power-driven individual mentioned above must face that part of her/himself that overrides awareness of the body, judging natural responses to stress as weakness. Shadow dominance does not value the welfare of the whole system. To evaluate both the positive and negative consequences of our choices provides a model through which we can more adequately examine our larger environmental context. If I can't resolve a conflict with a neighbor or a friend, how can I expect nations to resolve differences? If I haven't learned the value of my own physical body and its relation to the events of my life, how will I come to know the signs of a society overstressed and on the edge of sickness? If I expect to have whatever I want whenever I want it, how can I expect a slowdown in the devastation of the Rain Forest? Although our personal change cannot be expected to change all the problems in the world, there is some mysterious connection between individual behavior and the behaviors of our species as a whole. We do daily violence to ourselves, so we ignore the violence in our streets, or, the other way around, we desensitize ourselves to the violence that surrounds us and thus we ignore the mistreatment of ourselves. We don't see the connection between ourselves and the Rain Forest, so we destroy both.

Individuals keep the unacceptable parts of themselves hidden in the personal unconscious; our cultural shadow remains locked away in the collective unconscious. Just as we need self-reflection and personal responsibility for individual psychological health, our collective well-being demands social and environmental consciousness. Awareness of the personal shadow helps us take responsibility for ourselves and in turn offers new possibilities for collective behavior. There is a little story from the Hoopa tradition called "Humming Home Your Shadow" that gives us a mythic image for keeping connected to all the parts of ourselves. It goes like this:

> When you get up in the morning, Hoopa Indian children are told, it is very important for you to wait until you get your shadow home. When you go to sleep at night, part of you—your shadow—takes off. The part that you've held down all day, the part that you wouldn't let live. When you go to bed, your shadow says, "Now is my chance. I will go out and explore the world that you won't let me touch all day." And off it goes. The shadow has the freedom to go as far away as it wants to, but it has one tie: You have a hum that only your shadow knows. And it can never dis-

obey you. So when you get up in the morning, if you remember to hum, your shadow will come back home. Even though it doesn't want to. So when you get up, before you go out, give your own little hum, and your shadow will say, "Oh! I have to go home," and it will come home. And you are never ready for the day until you have taken time to sing the song of your own shadow. Some people say, "I must have gotten up on the wrong side of the bed—I think I'll go back and start over." They've forgotten to hum! Or some people get up at seven, and at ten o'clock they're still saying, "Don't mind me, I'm not all here." They've forgotten to hum! So there is a land of wisdom in remembering to get yourself all here every day. This is taught to the Hoopa tribal children not by saying, "When you get up in the morning you must do this!" but by saying, "Hum your song, so your heart and your spirit come together."[1]

This story points out that "there is a land of wisdom in remembering to get yourself all here every day." Our neglected parts eventually become our more destructive parts, not because they are innately negative, but because in separation we are divided in ourselves and can only bring partial responses to the events of our lives.

The mythology of the hero consistently places the shadow outside and names it "enemy." In pursuit of the demons, heroic consciousness uses the power of destruction and calls it justice. Like all aspects of life, the heroic stance has its own shadow. The shadow of preserver is

---

[1]Retold by Sister Maria Jose Hobday, "Humming Home Your Shadow," in *Parabola*, Winter, 1982, Vol. VII, #1, p. 23 (from the oral tradition of the Hoopa Indians of the West Coast).

destroyer. As we experienced in America's internal conflicts during the Vietnam War, the shadow of the heroic mythology can tear a nation apart. In those years the heroic-warrior-king lost its sheen and much of its saving powers. When myths begin to lose their meaning, society stutters. We sent our young men and women out to be heroes in a time when our ideas about the relationship between justice and destruction were not clear. Our warriors paid the price of a society in turmoil. If the archetype of the hero is to undergo transformation, each of us must integrate some part of this unleashed capacity for destruction. In this way there will be fewer enemies and less need for conquerors.

In Jung's model of the human psyche, we learn that everything contains its own opposite. The warrior holds the possibility of becoming the peacemaker; the creator may also be the destroyer; the one who wounds holds the ability to heal. On an everyday basis, this concept is not as complex as it seems. On examination, the person who is always so pleasant in the world of work is frequently the same person who is disconnected in his/her personal world. The kids and spouse of this "great guy" might have another story to tell. But, of course, those are the stories we don't tell. The obvious alcoholic or violent abuser are vivid examples of the shadow that we try not to see, but there are subtle shadow aspects in all of us. Mom may not have been publicly obnoxious; she just used alcohol to numb herself to life and relationships. Dad may not have been openly violent; he simply kept an emotional iron hand over the entire family—for their well-being, of course. Everyone has some negative component to his or her personality; the more obvious ones can be named while our subtle abuses escape examination. Life is more than skin deep. Each of us must meet the challenge of knowing our other side if we are to create a healthier way of being.

EXERCISE 9

GETTING TO KNOW THE SHADOW

1. The way to get to know your personal shadow is to look more closely at those things that you don't like in other people. Very often what you are rejecting in someone else is that part of yourself that you are trying to keep hidden. Keeping track of your negative reactions can tell you about your own negatives.

2. Take the time to read a book about the shadow. There are lots of them on the shelves that will give you plenty to think about.

3. Take the negative and threatening images of your dreams seriously. These are often the parts of the dreams that we leave out when we tell someone else our dreams. Don't change dreams! Pay attention to exactly what they say. Your shadow is there.

4. Take a threatening image from your dreams and build it up by making a collage. If there is a frightening person charging through your dreams, try to become more familiar with him or her by collecting a number of images from magazines and newspapers that remind you of this figure. Put these images together in a collage and meditate on what they say about you.

5. As you become more familiar with your shadow, imagine it magnified into the world around you, and you will begin to understand the implications of the collective shadow.

Once we begin to accept the personal shadow as real, as a part of every person's life, we also begin to deal with our collective shadow. One of the basic shadow issues of the

Western world is the one-sided attitude that we always have the right answers; we believe that what is good for us is good for the rest of the world. This may be an old habit coming out of the missionary zeal of our Euro-American heritage, but it is a habit that the world can no longer afford. Historically, the heroic price has been paid by the conquered. The native cultures of The Americas can testify to this today, as can native cultures around the world. Collective reflection, like self-reflection, requires that we include the negative possibilities of our behaviors. In this way we become more responsible for the world in which we live and social patterns begin to change.

As mentioned earlier, Taoism's changing symbol of Yin and Yang is possibly the clearest example of the embracing of opposites, but a story familiar from Euro-American childhood may be just as helpful. The tale of "Beauty and the Beast" exemplifies the coming together of opposites.

As you may recall, the story begins with a description of Beauty as the daughter of a widower who has just lost most of his material wealth and is forced by life's circumstances to move his family to the country. Beauty, one of six children, has two sisters and three brothers. Of all the children, Beauty is most like her mother in her love for the country.

From the beginning, we see the archetypal theme of the opposites of death and rebirth; the death of the family structure opens the doorway to a rebirth in the unknown land. Beauty's sisters complain about their fate, but Beauty joins her brothers in the work of creating a new life, and being bonded to mother, land and animals strengthen her.

Beauty's father plans a journey back to the city because he hopes to recover some of his lost wealth. The sisters ask him to bring back rich gifts so that they can return to their previous status. Beauty, on the other hand, asks only for a rose that would beautify the land. Symbolically, the rose is often an image for the Great Mother or the archetypal feminine. The mother that supports Beauty is more than her personal mother. The sisters scoff at what they see as a foolish request. In reference to death-rebirth, the sisters have not died and been reborn to something new, but are, indeed, holding on to dreams of what they used to be.

The father's journey is a failure, and he must return home empty-handed; the old ways are not going to be restored. In the metaphor of the story, it is at this point that the father becomes disoriented. (We, too, may experience feelings of being lost and uncertain as we work to discover the new life waiting to be born.)

Eventually, Beauty's father comes out of the dark forest and finds himself at the doorway to a great palace, the palace of the beast. At first, the father finds no one at home and is welcomed only by warmth and shelter. He knows nothing of the beast. When he has recovered and is ready to return home, Beauty's father remembers her request for a rose so he picks one from the garden. It is at this moment that Beast appears. Beauty's father is stricken with fear as he is confronted by the great Beast for trying to steal one of the roses from the garden. Hoping Beast would take pity on him, he told his story, ending with Beauty's request for a rose. When Beast hears the story of Beauty's request he offers to take Beauty in exchange for the merchant's life. Beast gives the merchant a chest of silver and tells him that he has three days in which to bring his daughter back to the palace. The merchant is to give Beauty the choice of whether or not she will come.

Now Beauty's father returns home carrying powerful opposites: he has a chest of silver, the beginning of the family's return to wealth, but he also has the request that Beauty go live with Beast. The only mention of heroic behavior comes from Beauty's brothers who want to kill Beast. Their response is short-lived as Beauty makes the choice to go to live at the palace. No matter how hard her father tried to change her mind Beauty insisted. She says to her father:

> "It is my fault that all this has happened to you, Father. I will stay with the beast. Surely he can't be as bad as you think. He has spared you and given us this treasure. My staying with him is a small price to pay for all his kindness."[2]

In this statement we see Beauty's ability to see the bigger possibility of her situation. She sees that Beast may, in fact, be more generous and kind than he is ugly and mean. Beauty's sisters think only of the silver and their desire to recover the past. The brothers want to destroy and overcome Beast through power and death. But in Beauty's behavior we see another way of approaching the beast. Beauty wants no part of her brothers' desire to kill Beast; she knows the fairness of Beast's behavior and places her trust in him. She also follows her own heart and allows her love for her father to help her make her choices. These same responses lie within each of us when we are faced with the beasts in our lives. Like the sisters, we might yearn for our old comforts, or like the brothers, we may insist upon the use of force. How often do we dare to be like Beauty—acting out of love and fairness while choosing to meet the beast that calls us.

We have much to learn from the figure of Beauty. Beauty's first response to meeting Beast is to think that he is frightening, but yet so sad and lonely. She is able to see beyond her fear, to a deeper truth within this creature with whom she is to live. Her concern is not for herself but for Beast. The coming together of opposites, as Beauty meets Beast, is reflected in Beauty as a moment of fear and compassion. The beast has no unkind words for either Beauty or her father. Instead he asks Beauty to stay with him and become the mistress of his magnificent palace. He makes

---

[2]This, and following passages, come from Marianna and Mercer Mayer, *Beauty and the Beast* (New York: Four Winds Press, 1978).

only one demand on Beauty. He asks that she always speak the truth while she is with him.

The merchant is given great riches by Beast as he leaves his daughter to begin her new life. Another movement from death to rebirth. Beauty's life in the country is gone and she is being reborn in a life without family, into the palace of where she is to reign. The opposites meet, the ability to live together is yet to be discovered. It is one thing to glimpse the beast within ourselves, or in someone else, but it is quite another step to embrace what is revealed.

Beauty slowly comes to know Beast. In one of their early conversations, she discovers Beast's sorrow over the fact that he has to hunt and kill to survive. She also comes to know that Beast is a wonderful storyteller and a magician. They become very close companions and every night before Beast leaves Beauty he asks her to be his wife.

> Beauty always replied the same way. "No Beast. I am sorry, but though you are kind to me and have treated me fairly, I can never be your wife because I do not love you."

Beauty speaks the truth that Beast demands. Could Beauty love him and be his wife? Her reply is always "No," but nonetheless Beauty does not try to leave Beast and she is happy in his presence. Yet there is more to Beauty's story than we know. Most of all she looks forward to the nights and the wonderful dreams that fill her sleep. Through dreams Beauty has access to another world. A world that reveals to her a beautiful prince and a voice that says to Beauty; "Look deep into other's beauty to find your happiness." In the dreams it is a woman's voice that speaks to Beauty. The theme of the deep feminine is carried forward through a dream figure who requires something of Beauty; but the information of the dream is not yet in Beauty's waking life. There are messages for all of us from the world

of dreams, but translating them to waking life is often difficult.

In a magic mirror, Beauty sees that her father is ill. She
asks Beast if she may return home to nurse her father back
to health. Beast agrees but tells Beauty that she must return
in three weeks because he cannot live without her. That
night Beauty has another dream. Again the woman appears
in the garden and says to Beauty:

> "How blind you are! I had hoped you would
> know that happiness comes from seeing what
> does not always lie on the surface. Some things are
> not on the surface at all."

The dream messenger is working to break into Beauty's
consciousness. Beauty's concern for her father draws her
home and she leaves her search for what lies below the surface of her awareness unattended. In the lives of each of us
the old pulls of family and early patterning are often the
roadblocks to further development. Beauty's sisters encourage her to stay longer with the family. Although Beauty
worries about Beast she remains with her father to keep
him happy. At night she once again begins to dream about
her garden. This time the dream image is different from any
other that Beauty has had before. The dream was of winter
and the sky was dark. In the middle of the garden Beauty
saw the Beast on the ground looking quite dead. Beauty
woke with a sense of dread and she thought to herself:

> "My poor Beast—how awful I have been to him.
> How could I have betrayed my promise when he's
> been so kind." She said good-bye to her father,
> and immediately held the mirror before her, wish-
> ing to be back at the palace.

At last Beauty begins to understand her dreams and the
voice of the old woman who has been speaking to her. She

realizes that her relationship to Beast is more important than the pulls and pushes of the family. She returns to Beast out of her love and concern for him. When Beauty first went to live with Beast, it was to save her father; now she goes to save Beast. Beauty found Beast on the ground, by the pond, just as she had seen him in her dream. As she embraces his weakened body, she tells Beast how much she truly loves him. Her words revive and transform Beast. The ending of the story follows:

> Before Beauty's eyes, he began to grow stronger. With each breath he took, his beastly appearance began to fade. Hearing his heart still beating, Beauty took some water from the pond, and wet his dry lips. But she pulled back in surprise, for her beast was gone and in his place the prince of her dreams lay in her arms . . .
>
> At last Beauty understood the mystery of her dreams. The prince and the beast were one, and her love had saved them both from their enchantment.

This tale finds its resolution in the unification of opposites when Beauty understands that the prince and the beast are one. What she saw in her dreams was in her presence all the time. We, too, must find the wisdom of our dreams and the guide that can point the way to finding the unifying principle to the opposing forces of our lives. Like Beauty, we have to feel concern, sorrow, and compassion for what we see as beast. For Beauty to recover the prince within the beast she must first break the patterns of her own adaptive behavior. To adapt to the needs of the family rather than following the voice of her dreams would have killed both beast and prince. We, too, must break the bonds of earlier adaptations to follow deeper wisdom. We leave behind the myths of role fulfillment that maintain the status quo in order to explore the myths of expansive possibilities.

William Doty, in his book *Mythography*, tells us that myths are the adjustive responses for individual and cultural solutions to problems which all human beings face.[3] Today the problems we face will begin to be met when we, like Beauty, stop adapting to what already exists and begin making the adjustments that will protect and enliven the world. Living myths for our future will include the themes of expanding love, following mysterious guidance, and embracing the opposites.

LOOKING AT CASES

Let's turn again to case material to gain insight into working with the shadow. Those behaviors we judge as negative in other people are often our own shadow, or rejected parts, seen in someone else. The ability to become self-reflective allows us to see ourselves through our response to others. If "he always," "she always," "they always" begins to change in the direction of "I think," "I want," "I respond this way when he does that," then we are beginning to take the shadow inside rather than placing it on other people.

The material shared here can be interpreted at a personal level and has been looked at in that light by the dreamers. The purpose is to examine these dreams for their archetypal reference and to ponder their meaning for the collective. For this reason, very little personal information about the dreamers is included, for each of these dreams might be available to any of us; we each have the possibility of living in relation to the archetypal realm.

The first client has been recording dreams for over twenty years. The five dreams presented here came in the last four years. There were others before this and there will

---

[3]William G. Doty, *Mythography* (Tuscaloosa, AL: University of Alabama Press, 1986), p. 28.

surely be more in the future. The dreamer, like Beauty, must continue to wonder at the meaning of these dreams and to search for the action that might be required.

DREAM ONE

A voice states that the third world war has started. It is different from what anyone has imagined. Mankind has declared war on the earth. The scary thing is: people are winning.

Dreams of this nature have the power to evoke questions that, when taken seriously, can lead us into a radical awareness of the fragility of life. Some of these questions are: What is this "voice" inside the human psyche that dares to make this statement? On what grounds does this voice base its words? Is this a voice that sees a truth the dreamer is not yet conscious of? Are we willing to listen to this voice inside ourselves? Can we accept the shadow image as it is evoked? What would it mean to take this dream seriously as a statement about our collective situation? What actions might arise if we were to take this dream voice as a speaker of truth?

DREAM TWO

I've been in medical school. I've washed out, couldn't hack it, it seems. I'm embarrassed, determined to go back, don't know if I can. Somewhere, I become aware that my main problem with medical school was environmental. A wetland got wiped out. I fought against that and tried to preserve it. For the school it was "business as usual."

The important statements of this dream, for the dreamer, were: "A wetland got wiped out," and, "for the school it was business as usual." On a personal level, the dreamer is asked to change his behavior, but what about this dream as applied to our collective situation? Hasn't the scientific medical model begun to destroy the quality of life for all of us? Haven't too many of us made the adaptation to business as usual without conscious awareness of consequences? A simple collective interpretation of this dream would be: when business goes on as usual, destruction becomes an environmental problem. Like the dreamer, we must all let go of our established orientations and find the adjustive response. We have to be willing to leave the known order to find the healing that can protect the environment. We must wrestle with the collective shadow of "business as usual" if the environment is to be preserved.

DREAM THREE

Statement in a dream: "If you are separated from nature, a problem cannot be separated from its solution."

Here we meet a dream that is like a riddle. Is this a nonsense statement, or does it penetrate into a deeper reality? This dream riddle tells the dreamer something about the way things work. Problem and solution are intertwined. Like Beast and Beauty, human and nature must come together. It is a challenge from the dream world to reconnect what is separated. When we listen to the wisdom of the dreamtime, our relationship to the world around us changes.

DREAM FOUR

There is a long line of Asian people extending toward the horizon. Underneath them, a long crack appears in the world. Golden yellow light issues from behind the crack. The people are all

filled with some kind of suffering. I know, somehow, that death is the passageway to the world of
the light, and that in that world is the peace which
"surpasseth all understanding." I know that relationship with this long line of suffering people is
the way of death—the necessary connection.

This dream had a strong religious feeling for the dreamer.
Suffering and death are balanced by the yellow light. The
apparent opposites of suffering and peace interface and the
dreamer knows he must begin to search for a consciousness
that can embrace the necessity of death; he must join the
suffering of the long line of people. The next dream helps
the dreamer make the leap.

DREAM FIVE

Someone who "knows," who "has been to the
other side," is talking. He says that we'll understand, someday, that it all makes sense. I ask him if
even the suffering of the world makes sense. . . . I
mean the suffering of Gaia, but also the suffering
of all the people of the world. He says yes, even
that will make sense.

This dreamer realized that it is important for him to move
more deeply into the suffering of the world. His training
had taught him a professional stance that held suffering at a
distance. Through increased self-awareness, the dreamer
expanded his collective awareness. This series of five
dreams was spread over approximately one year, with a
variety of other dreams between the ones shared here. The
important thing is that the dreamer records his dreams and
makes the connections between dreams over time. Forget-
ting the dreams and not seeing their relationship would be
the same as letting the beast die and never recovering the
prince.

Remembering dreams and integrating them into daily living helps us look at their collective implications. The archetypal psyche is the mythic psyche. Dreams grip the individual for personal development as well as to provide new insight into cultural patterns. One of the purposes of mythology is to connect the individual to the invisible world behind the visible world. By treating these words and images as though they had come from our own dream world, we can begin to see the connection between ego and soul, between person and world, between individual and the collective.

Dream One asks us to look at the war mankind has declared on Earth. Dream Two challenges us to examine the ways in which we attend to life as "business as usual" while destruction goes on around us. Dream Three speaks of our separation from nature and the relationship of problem to solution. Dreams Four and Five reveal the suffering of people and planet while suggesting meanings that we have yet to understand.

The beast of these five dreams requires a continual facing up to the destructive aspects of life. The prince of these same five dreams represents the formation of a new philosophy that can become a way of life for the dreamer, as well as for any of us. The dreamer, like Beauty, tries to understand the dangers and the magic of these dreams. In this struggle he is forced to make life choices concerning both work and leisure time. An involvement with nature, a connection to the suffering that surrounds him, and an active participation in protection of the environment are key to this individual's daily life. In this way, dreams and activities stay related and the dreamer finds life to be both meaningful and inspired. As this individual lives his dreams, he grows in mythic consciousness. We can all do the same.

The second client is a woman who frequently has dreams that reflect her growing connection to the archetypal guides of her psyche. Like Beauty, this dreamer is developing an intimate relationship with The Mother,

Earth, the Wise Old Woman who presents the threads of deeper understanding. We are all mythic dreamers, if only we make the time to relate to the material presented by the unconscious. Our conscious ego position is quick to dismiss dreams as meaningless or too ordinary to be worked with. We quickly forget dreams, or, if we remember them, we make a rapid interpretation that robs the dream of its potential. To meet the unknown world of our archetypal depths, we must embrace all that is presented—without judgment. The simplest image or statement from the psyche may hold the deepest meaning if we are willing to contain what is presented long enough for it to blossom.

The image shared here is presented in hopes of encouraging each of us to more fully embrace the world of dreams. This drawing (figure 8, page 120), came as the client worked with a series of dreams having to do with the theme of a journey into an underground cave. The dreamer had reached a point that felt like the bottom; the deepest, darkest part of her descent. At this moment the "goddess who weaves the universe" was there to provide a blessing for the next phase of this woman's journey. The blessing from this goddess helped the dreamer to trust this newly discovered world.

These two people, working at their particular versions of the myth of individuation, mirror for us the relationship to something in the psyche that is more than personal. It is important to remember that the tension of bearing the archetypal world is not an easy development. We are often required to include images of the center that may not be consistent with earlier ideation. If my god images have been those of a loving father in heaven, it is an enormous stretch to accept opposite images that may emerge from the unconscious. If I have long ago given up certain interpretations of the world, or of the divine, I will experience resistance and conflict when previously discarded images appear for reexamination. The developed ego suffers significantly in learning to embrace soul.

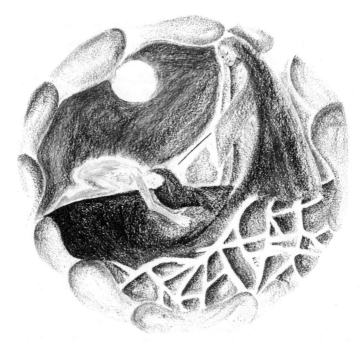

Figure 8. The Goddess who weaves the universe waits to be discovered within the human psyche. When we meet her, she will bless us. Illustration used by permission.

It is the ability to endure suffering at this level that breaks down our ego-centric patterns and leads us to a position of serving something more than our personal needs and desires. This mythological view of consideration for the whole is a cornerstone in religious traditions, as well as in social-political movements. In the Judeo-Christian tradition, concern for neighbor is paramount. In Buddhism, compassion leads to right relationship to others. In Islam, it is divine law that a religious tax, *zakat*, be paid to fulfill the obligation of charitable action. Concern for the common good is found in the ideation of Socialism, Communism, and Democracy.

Today, family, community, and country are being redefined on a global scale. When revolution breaks out in

China, the "former" Soviet Union or South Africa, the world watches. Access to information has changed everything. Our cultural coding keeps us thinking in specifics that are outmoded. It is no longer useful to think only of our own economy, our own land use, our own political beliefs. At the level of soul-work the adjustive response to a more complex world view is pushing to be discovered. We hold within us the ability to grasp whole systems and to discover the mythologies that guide us toward individual and collective wholeness—not a wholeness that we all squeeze into to be exactly alike, but a wholeness that is inclusive; not a wholeness that strives for perfection, but a wholeness that is able to hold the tension of diversity. Myths and cultures cannot be made generic to achieve wholeness. We have yet to develop the ability of individuals and cultures to include others while being themselves. We have yet to learn the myths that can bear the tension of living with difference and opposition.

One of the mythic paths open to us is the mythology of our original relationship to the rest of creation. We have looked at cases that reveal our connection to something that is personal and more than personal at the same time. At the level of the transpersonal we see a connection to other people, to the earth, and to the wisdom of the gods and goddesses. The mythic theme of our original relationship to the whole of creation is another major motif for cultural and personal development that can guide us to future becoming. We can return to mythologies of our beginnings to recover our original humanness and, in turn, our original connection to the sacred.

CHAPTER EIGHT

CREATION

We approach creation stories in the hope of finding lost knowledge about the origin and meaning of life's patterns. Creation myths are statements of beginnings; teachings about the mystery of how things came to be the way they are. In seeking understanding of the invisible world behind the visible world, there is no more important source than creation mythology.

Eliade calls creation myths "sacred history,"[1] Campbell describes Eden as "the garden of man's soul"[2] and von Franz suggests that myth is the language of the psyche.[3] These definitions return us to the truths of our beginnings—our relationship to the creator.

Creation mythologies have been trampled into meaninglessness in the Western world by the conflicts between science and religion. These meaningless arguments demand that one mythology be chosen over the other. Creationists, in their unwillingness to include science as part of creation, reflect as much disregard for the mythology of scripture as do research scientists. We must remember that myths are metaphors, teaching stories, roadmaps and symbolic statements. Although myths contain physical, spiritual and

---

[1]Mircea Eliade, *The Quest* (Chicago: The University of Chicago Press, 1969), p. 75.
[2]Joseph Campbell, ed., *Myths, Dreams and Religion* (Dallas: Spring Publications, 1970), p. 157.
[3]Marie-Louise von Franz, *C. G. Jung: His Myth in Our Time* (Boston: Little Brown, 1975), p. 217.

psychological realities, literal interpretations lead to a diminishment of mythic messages. In the Genesis story of creation, for example, the point is not how many days it took God to create the world. The point of the myth is that *we did not create the world* and thus we are not in charge of creation. Genesis reveals divine creativity and our human relationship to powers greater than our own.

Creation myths show us that "once upon a time" it was our natural condition to be part of transhuman creativity. These myths help us to understand how life works in the world around us as well as within the human psyche. They also provide non-heroic models for human behavior. There are no warriors or kings in the Garden of Eden. Paradise is that time when God is still at the center of the garden. Creation mythologies demonstrate our affinity with the creator and with creation. Rediscovering the heritage of myths about beginnings awakens a shared reality of existence. As Brian Swimme says in *The Universe Is a Green Dragon*:

> Most amazing is this realization that every thing that exists in the universe came from a common origin. The material of your body and the material of my body are intrinsically related because they emerged from and are caught up in a single energetic event. Our ancestry stretches back through the life forms and into the stars, back to the beginnings of the primeval fireball. This universe is a single multiform energetic unfolding of matter, mind, intelligence, and life. And all of this is new.[4]

---

[4]Reprinted from *The Universe Is a Green Dragon*, by Brian Swimme. Copyright 1984, Bear & Co., Inc., P. O. Box 2860, Santa Fe, NM 87504, p. 28. Used by permission.

This is "new" to modern science, but ancient in the imagery of mythology. Stories of creation often begin with narrations that express a sense of some mysterious "energetic unfolding of matter, mind, intelligence, and life." Through symbolic language, these early mythologies reveal the existence of active phenomena before creation, places where the world begins and out of which creation comes. These descriptions provide us with an awareness of the vastness of the forces of creation. In Norse mythology there is Ginungagap, the gaping pit between frozen fog and raging fire. In the Hebrew scriptures we find an earth "without form and void," with darkness over the face of the abyss, and a mighty wind over the surface of the waters. Hindu mythology speaks of the cosmic egg that emerges from the world ocean as a result of the friction between wind and water. Each myth calls into being energy-generating images of life before form: the powerful, mysterious, elemental forces of divinity.

These introductory portraits establish the human condition. We are the creatures—not the creator. Within the body of creation stories we find guidelines for human behavior and maps for relationship to the Holy Other that has created us. The true beginnings of creation mythology are our dependence upon the elemental forces of nature for our survival. We are water, air, wind, lightning. When these forces change, we, too, are changed. All premodern cultures know this. We, on the other hand, have lost sight of this reality through our separation from nature.

We speak of the natural world as though it were an object outside of us rather than seeing that we are contained in nature and part of it. We have taken the position that human beings have a reflective consciousness that sets them above the rest of the biological world. "I think, therefore I am," has become our motto. We assume that human beings are the only species with this reflective ability, and place ourselves as the authority over the rest of the natural world. To return to the mythic depths of creation stories offers us the opportunity to regain the ancient knowledge and to enliven our soul's connection to creation and the creator.

We have so misinterpreted the Genesis mythology that it is best to explore stories that are less familiar. In Aztec mythology from Mexico and Central America a story titled "In the Beginning" helps us to understand the relationships of creatures to creator:

> Alone was Tepeu, alone was Gucumatz, alone and wrapped in the green and the azure. All was silence, all was motionlessness, all was breathlessness. There was only the boundlessness of the sky, the quietude of the waters. No thing was joined to another thing; no thing was poised; no thing held itself upright. Lo, all was silent and unruffled; all was quietude and immensity. Then, wrapped in the green and the azure, Tepeu and Gucumatz meditated, and spake together and consulted. Then they were aware of the presence of him who is Heart of the Sky, who is Hurakan. "Let this and this be done," came the word to Tepeu and Gucumatz. "Let the waters retire so that the earth may exist. Let the earth harden its surface so that it be sown with seed. Let there be human beings endowed with intelligence so that from them we may receive glory and honour."[5]

The true purpose of the human being is immediately presented in this myth. The original intent of our existence

---

[5]This, and the material that follows, is from P. Colum, "In the Beginning," in *Orpheus: Myths of the World* (New York: Macmillan, 1930), p. 285ff.

and our intelligence is to "glorify" the gods. The purpose of the soul is to tend the holy; the purpose of the human is to serve the sacred. In the Western world, we have professed the purpose of our creation to be dominion over that which is not the same as ourselves—nature, territories, and other cultures. We have confused the original intent of glorification of the gods with glorification of our own power.

Fortunately, creation myths also guide us in dealing with our imbalances. According to the stories, the creator has had problems with the created from the beginning. Apparently, the newly formed humans do not fulfill their purpose. They are unable to speak the names of the Gods. Seeing the limitation of their creation, the Gods met in council and began to shape men from the substance of the Earth. These men of clay could stand upon their own feet, but could not move their heads or limbs. They could not lift their heads toward the Gods, and they could not speak out to honor them. These first people had meaningless speech, their sight was dim, and they could not move on their own accord. The Gods were unhappy with the men of clay and they broke them into pieces.

In examining this part of the myth, we are challenged to ask ourselves how, individually and socially, we are like the "men of clay." Do we stand upright, see dimly and speak words that make no sense? Do we model human behaviors that displease the Gods?

As the story continues, we see the Gods again reflecting upon their creation. This time the Gods determine to create men out of wood. These wooden men have speech, movement and the ability to reproduce themseves. The Gods watch as the Earth is peopled with their new creation. But these people, like those before them, do not raise their heads toward the Gods. They are a people without thought and memory; and they have no hearts. As the Gods watched them, they saw that these were not the people they desired. The Gods destroyed their creation once more.

The myth shows us not only what the gods desire, but how the human continues to fall short. The Men of Wood begin to fill the earth, but they do not raise their heads to the gods. We must ask ourselves: How is this true today? In ourselves? In our world? As we in the modern world have flourished, we have forgotten to acknowledge divine involvement. We, like the Men of Wood, have ignored the unseen world of the sacred creator. It is time to examine ourselves and see where we have no thought, no memory, no heart, and no blood. We must face how we bring about our own destruction.

Creation myths suggest that there is something within the human that diminishes the relationship to the divine. The Aztec gods resolve to destroy the Men of Wood. The same response comes from the god in Genesis who brings the flood to wipe men and beasts off the face of the Earth. The themes of creation and destruction are commonly held together within these stories. We discover patterns of ongoing cycles of creation, expansion, contraction, disintegration, and new creation. The fact that creation is not perfect from the beginning points out that we are not perfect, and that we go through many cycles of birth, growth, stagnation, death, and rebirth to accomplish the creation of our own lives.

Returning to the story, we learn that the Gods were still intent upon creating a creature who would glorify and honor them. In their determination, another cycle begins. Once more the Gods reflect upon their creation. The Gods send Crow and Coyote to the place where the waters divide, with instructions to return with white and yellow maize. With the help of Crow and Coyote, the Father and the Mother of the Gods make a series of nine broths that create the living substance of the first human beings. The men of maize are a new people who can stand and move, have sense and feeling, and can see clearly.

When the men of maize lifted their heads, nothing was hidden from them and they understood all that they saw. The Gods were astonished by this new creation, and they became afraid. The Gods feared that the men of maize would become their rivals. Although the men of maize lifted their heads to the Gods and gave thanks, their words did not soothe the creators. The myth comes to its conclusion as it tells us that the Gods respond to those people who can understand both Heaven and Earth by setting a limitation upon them. After all their labors, the words and the gaze of the men of maize made the Gods uncomfortable. The story concludes as follows:

> Then the Heart of the Sky breathed a cloud before the First Men so that their eyes were covered as with a mist. They saw, but they did not see clearly what was far nor what was near. Their vision and their wisdom became small—small as they are with us.

Another dimension is added here, not only to the creature, but to the creator. The gods work hard to create a creature that will worship and glorify them, but to do so they must give this new man the ability to speak, to understand, to think, to walk, to see far and near, to understand all things great and small, and to gaze upon both heaven and earth. The Gods, themselves, seem to be overwhelmed by their own creation, and thus cover what they have created with a mist. The human is left with a vague sense of vision and wisdom. According to this mythological approach, the basic condition of our creation is that we have yet to find a way to illuminate the wisdom and vision that lies behind the cloud that covers our eyes. The myth explains our limitation while, at the same time, suggesting possibilities of further development.

The similarity between the Aztec story and Genesis can be seen in the discussion between Eve and the serpent about the Tree of the Knowledge of Good and Evil. Eve says: "God has forbidden us either to eat or to touch the fruit of that; if we do, we shall die." The serpent said, "Of course you will not die. God knows that as soon as you eat it, your eyes will be opened and you will be like gods knowing both good and evil."

The creator Gods are ambivalent: they desire a creature who can enter fully into relationship with the whole of existence, while at the same time, they fear a creature who has the ability to see the whole. The human condition may be that we see only dimly into creation and are left with the struggle of William Blake when he says:

> The roaring of lions, the howling of wolves, the raging of the stormy sea, and the destructive sword, are portions of eternity, too great for the eye of man.[6]

In the Jewish tradition of the Qabbalah we find this archetypal idea of the divine-human relationship as closeness without clarity. It is thought that at the moment of birth, when the soul comes to Earth, an angel extinguishes the light of knowledge, and the soul, enclosed in its earthly envelope, enters this world having forgotten its lofty wisdom, but always seeks to regain it. The journey available within the tradition of creation mythology is the journey toward the sacred. The myths reveal the restraints of such a journey; they warn us of its dangers and encourage us to go forward.

These mythic themes of relationship to the sacred come in large cultural myths as well as more ordinary folktales.

---

[6]June Singer, *The Unholy Bible* (Boston: Sigo Press, 1986), p. 91.

Two tales from the Grimms' collection may help us to see the many faces of this relationship. These two tales warn of the dangers of inappropriate relationship to the greater Other that enters life. The first story is called "The Old Man Made Young Again," and tells us of a time when our Lord walked the Earth with St. Peter. The two stopped one evening at the home of a smith. While Jesus and Peter were in the smith's home, an old cripple came begging alms. St. Peter was moved with compassion for the old man and he said:

> "Lord and master, if it please you, cure his torments that he may be able to win his own bread."[7]

The Lord, too, felt compassion and was pleased with Peter's idea. He immediately went about building a larger fire in the smith's workshop, and said he would make this ailing old man young again.

> St. Peter blew the bellows, and when the coal fire sparkled up large and high our Lord took the little old man, pushed him in the forge in the midst of the red-hot fire, so that he glowed like a rose-bush, and praised God with a loud voice. After that the Lord went to the quenching tub, put the glowing little man into it so that the water closed over him, and after he had carefully cooled him, gave him his blessing, when behold the little man sprang nimbly out, looking fresh, straight, healthy, and as if he were but twenty.

At first this seems a simple healing story. But, as the story continues, it goes a step further. Apparently, the smith

---

[7]This, and the following passages, are from P. Colum, J. Campbell, J. Scharl, "The Old Man Made Young Again," in *The Complete Grimms' Fairy Tales* (New York: Random House, 1972), p. 640.

had watched everything very closely and after supper he began to wonder if he might be able to repeat what he had seen. Having an old mother-in-law who was also curious about what had gone on, the smith proposed that he might heal the old woman. The two entered into a plan to make the crooked mother-in-law young again. The smith began to heat up the coals. When he had a great fire burning he threw the old woman into it and she began to jump around and utter terrible cries of murder. The smith yelled to the old woman to sit still, and as he spoke, he built the fire even stronger and he blew the bellows until the old woman's clothes were burnt away. The old mother-in-law cried without ceasing, and the smith thought to himself:

> "I have not quite the right art," and took her out and threw her into the cooling-tub. Then she screamed so loudly that the smith's wife upstairs and her daughter-in-law heard it, and they both ran downstairs, and saw the old woman lying in a heap in the quenching-tub, howling and screaming, with her face wrinkled and shriveled and all out of shape. Thereupon the two, who were both with child, were so terrified that that very night two boys were born who were not made like men but apes, and they ran into the woods, and from them sprang the race of apes.

According to this folktale, the creation of lesser men is the outcome of taking on power that is not really ours. Although the work of the Lord appears to be similar to that of the smith, its difference is revealed in the two outcomes. In the beginning of the story St. Peter has compassion upon the old man. There is no mention of a similar attitude on the part of the smith toward his old mother-in-law. It is also important that St. Peter did not heal the man, but asked the Lord if it pleased him to heal the poor man. We, like the smith, may tend to think we can do what is in the hands of a greater authority. As the Lord was healing the old man, the story tells us that he was praising God. There is no mention of the smith's orientation to anything other than the skills of his trade. Inflation leads the smith to think of himself as more powerful than the saints.

Motivation is also at question in this tale. St. Peter's motivation for healing the old man was that he might be able to take care of himself in the future. The smith and the old woman are each motivated by personal interests. The smith wants to see if he can do what the Lord has done; and the old woman wants to be young again without suffering any pain. Here we are again confronted with the archetypal theme of right motivation. Like the story of "The Envious Neighbor" that we looked at earlier, we are reminded that the same action can lead to very different ends.

Another Grimms' tale, "The Ear of Corn," tells how human behavior toward the divine brings about particular outcomes.

> In former times, when God himself still walked the earth, the fruitfulness of the soil was much greater than it is now; then, the ears of corn did not bear fifty or sixty, but four or five hundredfold. Then the corn grew from the bottom to the very top of the stalk, and according to the length of the stalk was the length of the ear. Men however are so made, that when they are too well off they no longer value the blessings which come from God, but grow indifferent and careless. One day a woman was passing by a corn-field when her little child, who was running beside her, fell into a puddle, and dirtied her frock. On this the mother tore up a handful of the beautiful ears of corn, and cleaned the frock with them.

When the Lord, who just then came by, saw that, he was angry, and said: "Henceforth shall the stalks of corn bear no more ears; men are no longer worthy of heavenly gifts." The by-standers who heard this were terrified, and fell on their knees and prayed that he would still leave something on the stalks, even if the people were undeserving of it, for the sake of the innocent chickens which would otherwise have to starve. The Lord, who foresaw their suffering, had pity on them, and granted the request. So the ears were left as they now grow.[8]

We are warned against carelessness and indifference toward the abundance of creation. To hear the truth that is available within this simple story, we need only to think of its relevance for our modern society as it consumes the world's resources. Is not our chewing up Earth's forests to make paper plates similar to the woman's use of food to brush away dust? Both are blunders in the use of the blessings of creation. In remythologizing the world we must choose behaviors that establish a living relationship to creation.

The archetype of the hero-warrior-king has yet to be transformed within ourselves and within our culture. Creation myths declare the intent of the divine as something other than conqueror. We must remove the fog from our eyes and attempt to examine creator and creation as completely as we are able. In this seeing we will always be at risk of inflation and the misuse of creation. We may also acquire the much-needed humility that comes with the blessing of participating with creation. We must risk discovering the mythic depths of interconnection as

---

[8]P. Colum, J. Campbell, J. Scharl, "The Ear of Corn," in *The Complete Grimms' Fairy Tales* (New York: Random House, 1972), p. 791.

expressed in the following Rumi poem translated by
Coleman Barks:

A long cry at midnight near the mosque, a dying cry.
The young man sitting there hears and thinks,
"That sound doesn't make me afraid.
Why should it?
It's the drumbeat announcing a celebration!
It means, we should start cooking the joy-soup!"

He hears beyond his death-fear, to the Union.
"It's time for that Merging in me now,
or it's time to leave my body."
He jumps up and shouts to God,
If you can be human, come inside me now!

The signal of a death-yell splits him open.
Gold pours down, many kinds, from all directions,
gold coins, liquid gold, gold cloth, gold bars.
They pile up, almost blocking the doors of the mosque.

The young man works all night carrying the gold away
in sacks and burying it, and coming back for more.
The timid church-members sleep through it all.

If you think I'm talking about actual gold,
you're like those children who pretend that pieces
of broken dishes are money, so that anytime they see
pottery shards, they think of money, as when you hear
the word gold and think "Goody."

This is the other gold
that glows in your chest when you love.

The enchanted mosque is in there, and the pointed cry
is a candleflame on the altar.

The young man is a moth who gambles himself and
    wins.
A True Human Being is not human!
This candle does not burn. It illuminates.

Some candles burn themselves, and one another, up.
Others taste like a surprise of roses in a room,
and you just a stranger who wandered in.[9]

EXERCISE 10

TOUCHING THE WHOLE

General separation from the natural world leaves us isolated from the rest of creation. Endless hours spent in
automobiles and unfriendly work environments lets us
forget that we are part of a larger natural world. In regain-
ing our natural sense of wonder, we once again become
inspired by the facts of creation. Taking time to reconnect
to nature, as part of who we are, is a way of redefining the
collective as the world around us. To expand our awareness of environment, we can try doing the following
things.

1. Spend time outdoors every week. Meet and get to know
a few specific places on this planet.

2. Return to the same place often to see how it changes in
the seasons. Pay attention! Who are the plants, insects,
birds, animals, people, etc., that fill this territory? How do
they change or stay the same each time you return?

3. Later, when you're at home or some place where you
might find a quiet moment, use your imagination to recre-

---

[9]*Rumi Jelaluddin: We Are Three,* translated by Coleman Barks (Athens, GA: Maypop Books, 1987), p. 80. Used by permission.

ate this physical space you've been visiting. Remember its aliveness. Be aware of space beyond your daily routines. Recall the beauty of life around you.

A few other suggestions for reconnecting to the world around you are:

1. Take the time to walk or ride a bicycle instead of using your car.

2. Plant and tend a garden—even a flowerbox will do.

3. Put a birdfeeder in your yard, or outside your office.

4. Take your pencil and paper outside and spend time creating images of the life you encounter. Focus on one small leaf or caterpillar, drawing all the ins and outs of its individual form. Paying attention to the microcosm leads to insights into the macrocosm.

WORLD UNCONSCIOUS

In allowing ourselves to be drawn into the environments that we inhabit, we begin to experience nature as teacher—nature as healer. Stephen Aizenstat, in *Tending Your Dreams,* examines dream images for the voices of the world that come to us in moments of solitude. Aizenstat pushes psychology past the limited idea of the collective unconscious as a human-centered system, toward a more inclusive worldview. We are challenged to see and experience the psyche in nature as the world unconscious. He says:

> From the perspective of the World Unconscious, dream images are aspects of a world psyche, each image a part of a wider ecology of psychic life. Dream images of creatures, places, and things are

listened to as being sourced in the world psyche rather than being attributed to a personal or collective human experience. For example, when the dream image of an eagle presents itself, listen to the eagle speak of *its plight* in the world rather than so quickly connecting the dream image to your personal complexes or to a theme from a cultural myth.[10]

From the stance of the world unconscious, we learn to embrace phenomena as having movement and intentionality. The consequence of having lived too fully as heroic conquerors is that this narrow perspective has missed the enormous capacity of life around us. We are only beginning to realize that nature is more competent than we could have guessed. Just recently we discovered that "simple" woodland fungi are cleaning up human-created toxic dumps. Clearly, we haven't been listening to life around us. Yet, life is working full time to cope with the human species.

In reentering creation we begin to recover myths of relationship. Myths where consciousness is no longer defined as human centered, but as world centered. A myth where the human is part of a much larger cosmic story. A story that will help us understand what Teilhard de Chardin means when he says that the "supreme happiness" for human beings is when they find "themselves face to face with a unified universe."[11] A universe we joyously celebrate and to whom we sing the *Cosmic Chant* of the Takaroa Atoll:

[10]Stephen Aizenstat, "Tending Your Dreams," unpublished manuscript (Carpinteria, CA: 1993).
[11]Pierre Teilhard de Chardin, *How I Believe* (New York: HarperCollins, 1969) p. 16.

Life appears in the world,
Life springs up in the sacred land of the spirits.[12]
The Source-of-night sleeps below
in the void of the world,
in the taking form of the world,
in the growth of the world,
the life of the world,
the leafing of the world,
the unfolding of the world,
the darkening of the world,
the branching of the world,
the bending down of the world.[13]

[12]Meaning the Havaiki or ancestors.
[13]Barbara C. Sproul, *Primal Myths* (San Francisco: HarperCollins, 1979), p. 352.

CHAPTER NINE

CO-CREATION

Implicit within creation stories is the mythology of co-creation. Examples of human participation with the creator present themselves in the activity of Adam naming the animals in the Genesis story, and in African mythology where the cultural hero, Kaang, created the wild game and gave each animal not only its name, but its color and characteristics. In Norse mythology, like in the Aztec creation story, the Aesir Gods created the human for the purposes of worshipping the deities. Worship, in its wide diversity of forms, involves the actions through which the human assures divine participation in ordinary life. The gods are the life-givers and the humans assure survival through rituals and activities that please the transpersonal.

Human action becomes sacred action through its orientation to the gods and goddesses. Today, our actions have lost their sacred meaning and we no longer know our purpose of relationship to the invisible powers of creation. We have become like the monkey in the creation story of the Dahomey people of western Africa. In this story Mawu, the Mother of All, is the creator. In the beginning it was very, very dark. Mawu made fire and set in the heavens so that she might view all of her creation. In this new light, she found herself happy with all that She had made. Mawu called to monkey as he sat in a tree. She said to him:

> "Out of the clay I have formed you, breathed life into your earthen body; carefully did I shape

> your fingers and now the time has come for you
> to use them. From the clay you must form other
> animals. They may be of your own design, with
> feathers or with fur, with two legs or with four. I
> shall return to breathe the breath of life into each.
> When you have completed your task, you shall
> be rewarded well for I shall help you to stand as
> erect as the humans I have formed, so that your
> hands shall be free to use, even as you walk."[1]

Through implication of comparison we learn that the Goddess has created us, has breathed life into us and given us
movement, as well as the hands of creation. The monkey,
through the task of participating in creation, is offered the
chance to become like the humans.

> But when Mawu returned to see the work that the
> monkey had done, the monkey was not there. She
> stood before the pile of clay. Not a leg, not a
> feather—the clay remained as clay. The monkey
> had scampered off to brag to the other animals in
> the jungle of his great fortune-to-be. What use are
> hands, Mawu wondered, to one who only cares to
> twine his tail about the leafy branches and to boast
> to all his neighbors of what he has not yet accom-
> plished? What use are hands, Mawu wondered, to
> one who has allowed his chance to aid in the Cre-
> ation to slip by unfulfilled? Forever shall he
> remain a monkey and use his hands to walk. So
> Mawu then decreed—and so it has been for mon-
> keys until this very day.

---

[1]This and the following passage are from Merlin Stone, "Mawu," in *Ancient Mirrors of Womanhood* (Boston: Beacon Press, 1979, 1990), p. 137.

Like the monkey, we waste our chance to aid in creation. Our boasting and fascination with our self-importance leads us down the path of limitation. Nonetheless, there is also the opposite possibility: revitalizing a mythology of imagination and creativity that lies within the territory of the human personality.

In my previous book, *Illuminations: The Healing Image*, I help the reader uncover his or her own inner artist and creative spirit.[2] This time I find myself walking around the importance of carrying the myth of creativity in the culture. The creative aspect of society is enlivened when the artist within each of us participates in creative activity. It is the inner artist who helps us find the way to fulfillment. The inner artist dances on the continuum between self-absorption (the monkey's position in the last myth) and unity consciousness (the possibility offered by the creator goddess, Mawu). Imagination and creativity bridge the ego to the transpersonal. A bridge connecting the monkey of egocentricity to further development.

Our soul development is, in part, dependent upon recovering the mythmaking function within us. The artist carries myth forward in history, expressing the mythic dimension of culture. The artist within each of us touches the wisdom of the mythic deeps, engaging each of us in becoming mythmakers for a world that is always being recreated. To explore mythmaking within the creative spirit, I asked two artists to join with me in exploring creativity as they experience it, and to identify those points where the individual's creative expression meets the collective mythology of co-creation. The creative process is not limited to those we call "artist." The world of imagination and creation is shared by everyone.

---

[2]Madeline McMurray, *Illuminations: The Healing Image* (Oakland: Wingbow Press, 1988).

As an artist and a psychotherapist, I have the opportunity to walk in two worlds that are often foreign to one another. Although art and archetypal psychology are united in the realm of images, they often become alienated in the realm of interpretation. Images are as important to the psychotherapist as they are to the artist. A client's self-image, dream-image, parental-image are the primary material of the therapeutic process. Both artist and psychotherapist would be helpless without the images of the psyche.

While psychology brings an analytic evaluation to the world of images, it does not always include an aspect of participation. Too often therapist and client distance themselves from the power of the images of the psyche. Art, on the other hand, involves participation, but often includes an

Figure 9. Like Monkey, we have the opportunity to participate in creation; to be co-creators. Like Monkey, we must choose. From Geoffrey Williams, *African Designs from Traditional Sources* (New York: Dover, 1971), p. 82.

unwillingness to evaluate issues of meaning and cultural context. Our challenge is to discover the common ground between participation and evaluation. Ideas of objective/analytic vs. subjective/expressive can be transformed into more inclusive attitudes of interaction and interrelatedness. Object and subject can come together as well as be pulled apart, for ongoing creativity and differentiation. Cosmos out of chaos includes both creation and transformation.[3]

ON MAKING ART

One way we have of examining how objectivity and subjectivity interact is through looking at the artist and the process of creative expression. Wherever new creation is at work we find the artist. Whether it's a painting, a new research design, a poem, a piece of music, a new scientific discovery, a sculpture, or a breakthrough in genetic engineering, the creative spirit is in motion. As the artist works to bring the uncreated into being, there is a direct exchange between ego and soul. Within the creative process is the experience of something that is more than personal. As personal and transpersonal interweave for the purposes of co-creation; boundaries between subject and object blur.

Is the artist the objective human working on a subjective creation, or is the artist the subjective human being worked on by the objective creator? Although, there is no "correct" answer to this line of questioning, we are slowly coming to understand that definitions of objective and subjective are perspectives that cannot be separate from one another. Everything in the end is interactive.

In examining the process of making art our first example comes from Charlie DiCostanzo, an artist and professor.

---

[3]Madeline McMurray, "A Window Into Psyche," in *Psychological Perspectives* (Los Angeles: C. G. Jung Institute, 1989), p. 88.

Figure 10. The images of nature inspire creativity. With relatedness to the "muse," the artist becomes the vehicle for the spirit. "Waterfall." Wood and lacquer sculpture, Charlie DiCostanzo, Humboldt State University, Art Department. Illustration used by permission.

Charlie and I have spent many long evenings speculating on how the process of making art actually happens. We agree that a mythology of creativity lies hidden in the "doing" of artistic expression. The human and the divine come together in co-creation to form the unknown new life.

Charlie's recent work has been a series of lacquered sculptures based on the forms of nature. His subjects include waterfalls, lakes, mountains, and islands. Each piece stands on its own and needs no analysis, but through these works we can explore what happens in the process of making art. What is the procedure? Here are a few ideas from the artist's practice that may speak to each of us of the possibility of fully entering into a mythic position of co-creation, i.e., interacting with something that is more than one's personal ego position.

Charlie begins his explanation of art by starting with the "muse" as his source of inspiration. In Greek mythology the Muses are the nine daughters of Zeus and Mnemosyne who preside over art and science, and who inspire mankind. They are the creative spirits or inspirations that guide the artist at work.

Once the creative spirit is acknowledged, the next step is to create a space where the muse might enter. Charlie calls this the "ritual of preparation." He may put his tools in order, straighten up his studio, lay materials out in a particular way, get his cup of coffee. He is taking care of the details that form the space in which the creative work takes place. Part of the ritual usually includes a period of time for "false starts," moving first in one direction, then another. He may wander from one approach to another; there may be a time of indecision—not quite sureness—and then the direction of the work begins to take shape.

We must be willing to make mistakes and practice regularly as part of the ritual of preparation. There is no guarantee that we will be filled with inspiration every time we desire to be creative. The more we practice the more readily the creative state becomes available.

The creative state, the openness to inspiration, becomes known when the artist is fully engaged in the creative process. In these moments there is an experience of something moving through the person into the materials. The creation begins to take its own shape. The ego, in its receptivity, has surrendered to an awareness of creative energy that wants expression. The artist becomes the vehicle for the spirit.

This work is done in what Charlie thinks of as being outside time. He experiences timelessness through total involvement in the moment. This complete engagement is important to creativity. It is the moment when the human reaches into mythic time to interact with the archetypal psyche. This interaction requires complete focus and letting go of control—difficult but not unattainable. The ego moves to a position of observer rather than trying to be the ruler. Involving ourselves in co-creation teaches us to move past our ego and to open to something greater than the personal self. Through preparation, practice, receptivity, surrender, focus, and the muse, the artist in each of us can enter the larger realm of psyche to experience and express creative energy.

The limitations we feel about the inner reaches of our being are the result of ego-centered development. It may take time to open the doors to creative capacity, but it is time well spent—we are investing in our own development and in creation. The artist within us has the opportunity to participate in an exchange with the rest of life. Charlie likes to think in terms of "sympathetic magic," an exchange of energy between the artist, the creation and the rest of the universe. Charlie experiences a sense of reverence and respect as he works. He believes that his attitude contributes, not only to the making of a particular piece, but to the energy of the whole system in which he lives. Every movement of the hand moves molecules to the end of the universe and every act of creating has an effect. For Charlie, this invisible effect may be even more important than what is made visible.

These experiences of participating with the creative spirit of the universe, of reverence and respect for the rest of creation, lead to an understanding of our place in the whole of creation. We are co-creators, but in the face of this larger perspective, we are but grains of sand. Life, as a whole system, is creative and relational. Our task is to learn how to become more expansive in our participation.

Another artist, Meinrad Craighead, is a painter who lives and works in the desert of New Mexico. Although Meinrad's work is very different from Charlie's—one being a painter, the other a sculptor—her process of making art is surprisingly similar. Meinrad, like Charlie, has her "rituals of preparation" with the beginning of each day. In her book, *The Litany of the Great River*, Meinrad shares words and images of her morning fire-building ritual. She says:

> When I approach my altar in the dark before dawn, before I lay the cottonwood kindling and light the fire, I take ashes from yesterday's fire and rub them on my forehead (if every day is Resurrection, every day is Ash Wednesday). By the time I have made my sacred prayer circle, the fire has burned to embers. I end my prayer with water. I baptize myself. I say, "Meinrad, you are sealed. You belong to God. You drink her milk and her tears and you shed her blood. She looks at you. Because she looks at you, you paint." I throw the remaining water into the dying fire to hear the sound of the union and watch steam fill the belly of the vessel. Before long, in this high desert climate, the ash is gray dry, the bed for tomorrow's fire.[4]

---

[4]Meinrad Craighead, *The Litany of the Great River* (Mahwah, NJ: Paulist Press, 1991), p. 14.

Within the experience of making art, the artist opens herself to the movement of the creative spirit. With the dawning of each new day, Meinrad wonders how she will receive and what she will make. We can see in this artist the desire for transpersonal guidance as she works. The individual ego position is intentionally set aside for the greater purposes of creation. The artist is co-creator, cooperating with what calls for incarnation.

Along with her rituals for greeting the day, Meinrad maintains seven altars in her studio where she brings a deepening sense of the sacred to her work. The religious attitudes of awe, respect, and regard for the divine other-ness of creation are a part of Meinrad's daily approach to her painting. These attitudes are reflected in the naming of her studio after the Goddess Maat, the All-Seeing Eye of the Mother. Meinrad says of her studio work:

> I paint within her eye and she watches me. What more may I say of this Mother than, she keeps an eye on me. As her eye gives birth to me, my eyes bring out my images. The feather of her flying eye, seeking truth, falls on my brush. I built this space, this place, to encircle the eye of her presence. This is our home. This is it, my cell, where I live alone with her.[5]

In living with the All-Seeing Mother, Meinrad is living the mythology of co-creation. The artist acts as partner with the creative other that moves through life. We, like the artist, have a part to play in future creation. It begins when we open our consciousness to the energy of the creative spirit. Meinrad shares with us her experiences of the creative as it moves in the world that surrounds her. The muse comes to Meinrad as she listens to the music of Mahler, as she walks along the river that flows near her home, as she paints and

---

[5]*The Litany of the Great River*, p. 4.

even as she sleeps. Meinrad is aware that guardian angels hover over the birth of each new painting and she experiences painting as an act of worship. She quotes Plato: "Praying is painting and painting is praying."

Art is a sacred activity and through the artist all of creation is constantly being renewed. As Meinrad creates, she watches the invisible powers become visible through her. The paintings themselves become visions of the images of the divine treasure that resides within life. Meinrad describes the artist as a "see-er." She says:

> I don't think only artists are seers, or that a seer has to be an artist. Possibly great souls who "see" for the rest of us go down and bring back the treasure. As an artist, I'm the first to see the treasure which has never existed before. But the treasure is never for yourself. You are just the agent to receive it and bring it back.[6]

The artist fulfills a role for society by bringing mythic images into consciousness. What the artist sees is made flesh for all of us. Art is both an individual and a collective experience.

As we are touched by the artist's work, we become aware that we too are seers. There is a tendency to think that this creative spirit moves for others, but not for me; projecting onto the artist that they can do what we cannot. We will have to give up this excuse and explore the mythology of creativity that runs through the lives of all of us.

Both Charlie and Meinrad turn to nature as their model, guide, and source of inspiration. Mountains, rivers, earth images of many kinds speak to these artists, wanting to be expressed. Meinrad often has dreams of the places in nature where she spends time—the river and the desert.

---

[6]Pythia Pey, "Making the Invisible Visible," an interview with Meinrad Craighead in *Common Boundary*, Nov/Dec 1990, p. 20.

Figure 11. Paintings themselves become visions of the images of the divine treasure that resides within life. "Crow Mother over the Rio Grande," painting, Meinrad Craighead, Albuquerque, New Mexico, 1988. Illustration used by permission.

She dreams of guarding the space and somehow maintaining its wild sacredness. For Charlie, dreams are often the beginning of a new sculpture. The artist is both a seer and a dreamer, who sees his/her dreams and makes dreams seen. At the mythic level of the psyche we are all dreamers, seers, and artists. We may not express ourselves in painting or sculpture, but nonetheless we each hold some connection to the invisible power that desires to come into being through us.

To have insight—sight into—is a human ability that all of us are able to attain when we make the developed ego position secondary. When ego is primary the seeing may be present but the interpretation is from the personal perspective rather than from the muse or creative spirit. The artist, as model, reveals to us that we are wasting a great opportunity if we use insight simply to look at ourselves. Psychologically, we have the ability to see who we more truly are, how to live our lives more fully and how to work toward our own healing. We can also see into a vision for the collective to become more truly what we are all meant to be, to develop a meaningful quality of life that applies to the social order and to discover an existence that brings collective healing. The artist teaches us that without inspiration and vision there is no new creation. Without creativity there is no future.

THE ARTIST AS MYTHMAKER

We must not leave creativity projected onto the artist. It is important that we each, in our own way, become artists. There is room for creative expression in all dimensions of life. Learning to maintain a friendship or finding wonder in tending a garden can be expressions of a living myth of creation. The creative possibility can be found in all the moments of our lives. Life as sacred creation enables us to

be fully involved in the ordinary activity of daily living. As
a simple Zen story says:

> Before you study Zen
> a bowl is a bowl
> and tea is tea.
> While you study Zen
> a bowl is no longer a bowl
> and tea is no longer tea.
> When you are enlightened
> a bowl is again a bowl
> and tea is tea.[7]

As with the artist, the Zen monk experiences life through
seeing. We, too, have this capacity to see life as it presents
itself. The indigenous people of Columbia tell us that we
should not cut trees because it would bring the trees pain.
We interpret this as primitive madness. How could trees
feel pain? Yet is it possible that we "see as through a glass
darkly" and that we don't understand this intricate net-
work we call life. We could be changed by learning the
mythological views of other cultures and by looking more
deeply into our own.

The mythic depths either become part of conscious living or they wander aimlessly through the unconscious
landscape of our lives. Consciousness requires responsibility to and for the myths we live. Unconsciousness allows
myth to form our personal and collective history without
accountability.

On a practical level, in this age of information, the tools
of consciousness are no farther away that the nearest library
or bookstore. On the level of "how-to," it is important to
acknowledge that the primary ingredient in discovering

---

[7]Peter Montagnon, producer. "The Land of the Disappearing Buddha," from *The
Long Search with Ronald Eyre* (London: British Broadcasting Company, 1977),
Time/Life films.

our mythic depths is the element of time. We must find (*make*) the time to do the work of psycho-spiritual development. Not tending the psyche is an indulgence that we can no longer afford. To lose creativity is to stagnate and die. The theme of the artist as mythmaker is important to us individually as well as to the collective. To wait for society to change will be to wait too long. Society is made up of individuals. We, the individuals, hold the inherent ability to consciously connect to the mythic level of our existence. Change in ourselves and change in the world are interactive. Those people that we think of as the "great individuals," e.g., His Holiness the Dalai Lama, Mother Teresa, Carl Jung, Etty Hillesum, Thomas Merton, Albert Einstein, Sojourner Truth, to name only a few, are at bottom only human beings. Greatness lies within the soul of each person. It is the individual's connection to the structure of the universe. We have only to give up our inflated ideas of perfection and risk discovering the mythic deeps that desire expression.

EXERCISE 11

RITUAL AND ATTITUDE

We must regain our images and relearn our stories. Before finishing this book, spend time exploring your relationship to your creative self. The following exercise and suggested readings are placed here to help.

Activities like tending your dreams, journal writing, image-making, meditation, and breath work are all roads to finding the creative spirit that moves through life. The attitude of the artist as described in this section is an attitude that you can bring to the activity of your choice. The function of ritual is to bring myth into being. Design your own rituals of preparation for doing your creative inner work.

1. Create a space; i.e., table and chair, a desk, a sofa with good lighting—a place where you are comfortable.

2. Be consistent in using this space. Keep your tools—your journal and pen, your art materials, your computer in this space.

3. Each time you approach your space, establish an attitude of focus and reverence about what you are doing.

4. Rituals can be as simple or as elaborate as you like. Again, be consistent. Lighting a candle, saying a prayer or affirmation, or listening to a piece of music are all ritualistic ways of inviting the muse to join you.

Note: Allow that you will have false starts. Be willing to return to the same material more than once. Be receptive to what might come to you over time.

RESOURCES

Four resources that I'd like to point to as helpful guides for personal/archetypal work are:

Inner Work by Robert A. Johnson
Your Mythic Journey by Anne Valley-Fox & Sam Keen
Illuminations: The Healing Image by Madeline McMurray
The Miracle of Mindfulness by Thich Nhat Hanh

These books are clearly not the definitive work on the topic of personal development. There are hundreds more that are equally helpful. These four used together provide an excellent base for taking on the task of connecting to our deeper possibilities. Johnson gives a framework for working with dreams and active imagination. Keen and Valley-Fox use the tools of writing and storytelling for self-understanding, as well as understanding of the larger Self. I provide tools for the recovery of imagery and the inner artist. Thich Nhat Hanh teaches meditation as a daily activity in the events of our lives.

The tools and techniques available today are multiplying so rapidly that it is impossible to keep up with them all. It is helpful to establish one's personal focus and follow a chosen path long enough to experience some degree of integration. Leaping from technique to technique is often an interesting way of avoiding the demands of the mythic psyche. Staying on the surface is more comfortable and keeps our experience controlled by the ego. Integration requires a willingness to be changed by the otherness of life. The images, the dreams, the stories, the myths, and the events of daily life present themselves to us for response. We embrace and meet them, or we watch them pass.

LOOKING AT CASES

An example of a woman working with her dream may help to illustrate how staying with one thing for a period of time can lead to deeper and deeper development. This woman has a dream about the office where she works and the people that she works with. She begins by remembering the dream. She writes it down. She thinks about the dream and wonders about herself as well as the people and the place in the dream. Later she takes this particular dream to her therapist, where they explore her relationship to her work and the people in the dream. The dreamer explores what the dream wants to tell her about the different aspects of herself reflected in the images. Later she writes further on the dream and ponders its possible messages.

As her personal understanding of this dream changes, the dreamer begins to feel that this dream is speaking of more than her personal inner world. It is also about her workplace and her colleagues. She photocopies the dream and suggests that the group she works with meet to discuss the possibilities of what this dream may be saying to all of them.

The groups meets and begins to talk about the images of the dream. One image is that the waters are rising dangerously high around the building. With the help of this image the group can choose to look at issues they may have been avoiding: issues that may be getting "dangerously high" because they have been left outside the door. Through this work, not only is the dreamer changed, her colleagues also have the opportunity to be touched by the dream.

The idea of a dream being something for one's community is not uncommon. *Black Elk Speaks*, for example, is a book that reveals the dream process for the individual and the community.[8] Jung, when he was in Africa, was delighted to watch the bushmen sharing their dreams at the beginning of each day. The mythology of the dream is an invaluable resource for living one's life. To do it well, and to benefit fully, requires a commitment to listen to dreams and images consistently over time, and the willingness to leave the meaning of the dream open for continued revelation.

Working in this open way with dreams is another mythology of participation. We are co-creators interacting with the dreamtime. We relate to them or let them die. We bring them into consciousness or leave them in the darkness. The energy for further creativity lives in every dream. We have only to see it. I must restate that we are all dreamers, seers, artists, and storytellers. Through this development we become participants in the possibility of new discovery and new becoming, not only for ourselves, but for the world in which we live.

---

[8] J. G. Neihardt, *Black Elk Speaks* (New York: Pocket Books, 1972).

CHAPTER TEN

HEALING
THE HERO

The ties that link the many souls of the human species live in the realm of dream, vision, and myth. When the dreams, visions, and stories of a culture are lost, that society begins to die. In the aboriginal traditions of Australia and New Guinea, it is believed that if one loses the stories, the "song-lines," there is a break in connection to the land and to the people that threatens the well-being of the society.

As scientific-rationalism began to dominate the Western world, our mythology turned to ideas of objectivity. As linear models were established, the humanities adapted to artificial standards. At the end of this century we see the pendulum beginning to swing in a new direction. An openness to the idea of remythologizing our lives is apparent in the enormous interest in the works of Jung, Hillman, and Campbell. We are beginning to retrieve what the aboriginal cultures were never willing to give up.

People desiring inclusion of the mythic dimension in their lives often find that they cannot return comfortably to the old patterns of their upbringing. New myths and rituals must evolve in ways that are meaningful within our present context. Reconnecting to our mythic selves requires the willingness to search and explore the unknown territory of collective consciousness—that place where psyche speaks to and through each of us. In recovering mythology for modern living it is important that we not fool ourselves and simply engage in yet another heroic battle against the hero. Focusing on mythic themes of healing and transformation while letting go of heroic goals is best for now. Examination of the following Hopi myth helps us understand how to move the hero from his position of slayer. This is a story about the Twin War Gods and their Spider Grandmother. It is said that one day the boys decided to go into the valley to play a serious game. Their Spider Grandmother told them not to go into a place south of their home because it was not safe. The two War Gods climbed out of their kiva and went down the south side of the mesa and pondered their grandmother's warning.

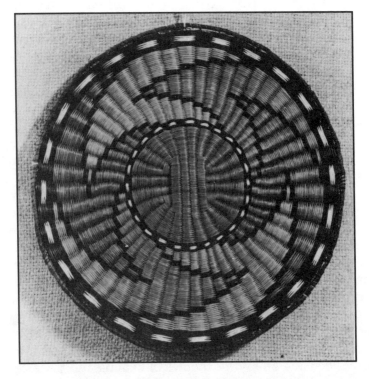

Figure 12. Whirlwind. Hopi Plaque E 1432, Museum of Northern Arizona Anthropology Collections. Used by permission.

They were certain that nothing could be that dangerous. They weren't scared of anyone out there. The twins hit the ball back and forth for most of the morning and became so engrossed in the game that they didn't notice where they were. The youngest one, Palongawhoya, thought to himself, "I'm really going to hit this one out of sight and see what my brother will do." As he thought it, he did it.

The two brothers ran to fetch the ball, but before they could move, the ball came flying back to them from the other side of the hill. The War Gods were amazed because they were sure that no one could hit the ball as well as they did.

> Their curiosity made them forget the warning they had received from their grandmother, and they hurried over the hill to see who could have such skill as to equal theirs. They beheld a large cornfield in which the corn stood high over their heads. They entered the field to look for someone. As they peeked from row to row, they suddenly came face to face with two young maidens whose beauty wiped away any sense of caution their grandmother hoped the boys would pick up from her warning.
>
> Eager to show their skill with the ball, the two boys suggested that they play a game. The maidens thought for a moment, and then accepted the invitation to play. But first, they wanted the game to be worthwhile; the winners should cut off one leg of each loser. To this the two boys agreed without hesitation, knowing that no one else had even been a match for them.[1]

---

[1] This, and the rest of the story that follows, is from S. Trimble, ed., "Hopi— Wunuuqam: Ones Who Stand," in *Stories from the Land*, published in *Plateau*, Vol. 53, #2, pp. 18ff (Flagstaff, AZ: Museum of Northern Arizona Press, 1981).

We have become like the twin heroes in this story. We know no bounds, we see ourselves as invulnerable, and we take no warning seriously. This is the position of the developing adolescent, not the position of an adult. In the story the War Gods are boys. Their behavior is predictable for boys. A reflective adult would want to listen to the warning of the Spider Grandmother. Even if one hadn't paid attention to the original warning, what quality is it that ignores the stated consequences of entering this game? The hero identifies with one side of power—the side of winning. This one-sided attitude is the beginning of trouble. Fascination with power gives the heroic personality a false sense that winning will always be the outcome. The grandmother's warning falls silently into unacknowledged possibilities.

As the story goes on the heroes find themselves in a much more difficult game than expected. By mid-afternoon the maidens win the game and quickly remind the War Gods of the prize.

> Now the boys were more concerned about what their grandmother would say for having ignored her instructions than they were about the consequences of their agreement with the maidens. In any case, what was done, was done. The maidens did their gruesome deed.
>
> As the sun was about to set on top of Apoonivi, the two started their journey home. First, they had to devise a way to move their maimed bodies along the trail. . . . They finally worked out a way: they would stand side by side with each unsevered leg on the outside. In this position, one could lean on the other for balance and support, and the other could lift him forward a distance of one step; then the two would reverse their roles. It didn't take long before they got the hang of it, and they were moving along almost as

one man walking, each also carrying his own sev-
ered leg as best he could.

Spider Grandmother was disappointed in what the boys
had done, but she immediately prepared to help them. She
made her medicine and reattached the boys' legs. She sang
her healing songs and the Twin War Gods were made
whole. Here we see the Spider Grandmother as a symbol
for the power of healing. Despite our destructive behaviors,
we can return to her and still be made whole. This mythic
understanding supports the transformation of the heroic to
a more balanced position.

No sooner were they whole before they wanted to
go right back and show the maidens that this time
they would win the game. Grandmother Spider, of
course, would not hear of it. But realizing that the
boys would go back against her will at the first
chance, the Spider Woman decided to tell the boys
that if they must go, they should take a certain
medicine which she promised to prepare in the
morning.

The desire of the hero to keep pursuing the challenge is more
powerful than the wounding. The myth reveals how difficult
it is to change heroic behavior. We must be as patient as Spider Grandmother while trying to provide the right cure. In
the morning, Grandmother Spider gave the boys an herb to
chew if they should need protection. She also suggested that
they take their bows and arrows with them when they go. Of
course, the heroic boys go directly to the cornfield in hopes
of engaging the heroic maidens in another ball game. The
twin warriors are determined to win, and the maidens are
determined to punish them in an even more gruesome way
than before. With these two attitudes, one about competition,
the other about revenge, the game goes on for hours and
hours. In a moment of surprise the boys win the game.

The War Gods can't bring themselves to the task of cutting off the legs of the two maidens, so they foolishly suggest a new game, a bow and arrow competition. When the maidens bring out their bows and arrows, the War Gods are shocked to find that these two young women have the finest bows that they have ever seen. Again, we see the hero's inability to evaluate situations in which he readily engages.

The competition went on for the rest of the day. They continued to move further and further into the territory about which Spider Grandmother had warned them. Rather than heed the warnings, our young heroes kept moving deeper and deeper into the area of danger. It was getting late and neither side had gained any advantage. They shot their arrows over the wall of the cliffs.

> When they reached the edge they looked down a steep cliff and felt dizzy; their arrows were somewhere out there away from the foot of the cliffs. Now the twin War Gods remembered the herb medicine that Spider Grandmother had given them. Quickly they chewed on the herb to mix it with their saliva, and then each one spat down the cliff wall. As soon as they did this, they jumped down. They came down sailing and tumbling, but as they neared the ground of soft sand they seemed to slow down and their bodies turned upright as they landed softly on their feet unhurt.
>
> They looked up at the maidens who were still standing at the edge looking down. They beckoned to the maidens to jump down and to not be afraid. But the two maidens were obviously too afraid to jump. No matter how hard the boys coaxed, the maidens refused. Then one brother turned to the other and said, "Well we must now spit our medicine up to them, for that

is what they are asking for." As he said this, they spat their medicine up to where the maidens stood, side by side. The maidens immediately turned into two stone columns. The twin War Gods picked up their arrows and returned home to Grandmother Spider with a story about a great game.

The games of the War Gods with the maidens from the south may have never ended if it had not been for Spider Grandmother's medicine. Involved in endless competitions, the heroes ignore all danger. Warriors often pursue winning over paying attention to the truth. In the beginning of the story the Spider Grandmother tells the twins that the south is a dangerous territory. She tells them that it is unsafe and that they should not play there. The grandmother has knowledge of what is true, knowledge that the heroes ignore.

Fortunately for these twins, Spider Grandmother's medicine intervenes in their game. The maidens, no matter how attractive, are in fact dangerous. The War Gods had no intention of stopping the competition. They spat the herb up to the maidens to keep the games going. The medicine of Spider Grandmother had its own purposes—healing and protection. Apparently the twin War Gods have to be protected from themselves. Without the protective medicine they might still be with the maidens in the dangerous land of the south.

Haven't we all, at one time or another, experienced the intervention of the Spider Grandmother? We are headed in one direction when some outside force seems to step in and change everything. We believe that life is under our control until an accident or an illness makes it impossible for us to continue at our same pace. Or we're looking for a particular professional placement when, through one connection or another, we find ourselves interested in doing something that we'd never considered before. Or we take a vacation, fall in love with a complete stranger, and move halfway across the nation to be with a new lover. These may, in fact, be interventions of the Spider Grandmother and her medicine.

Another story about healing the heroic-warrior comes from *The Pine Gate*, by Thich Nhat Hanh. In this story we learn about the importance of seeing clearly.

It was a cool, almost chilly, autumn evening, and the moon had just risen, when the young swordsman arrived at the foot of the mountain. The wilderness was bathed in the light of the full moon glimmering playfully on branches and leaves. It seemed to him that during the seven years he was away, nothing in the surroundings had changed. Nothing had changed, and yet nothing seemed to be greeting him with any warmth—he who had once lived there for years, and who was now returning from afar.

The swordsman paused at the foot of the mountain and looked up. Above him, the narrow path was barred by a pine gate which was tightly shut. He pushed at the gate's sturdy doors, but these remained immovable under his powerful hands.

He was puzzled. Never, as far back as he could remember, had his Master had the gate closed and locked like this. Since this was the only way up the mountain, he had no choice. Slapping the handle of his sword, he rose swiftly from the ground. But that was all. A strange force gripped his whole body and pushed it back down; he could not jump over the low gate. In a moment, he had unsheathed his long sword, but the sharp blade bounced back from the soft pine wood as if the latter were steel. The impact was so powerful it sent a shock through his hand and wrist. He raised his sword and examined its gleaming edge under the moonlight. The gate was indeed too hard; most certainly his Master had endowed it with the strength of his own spirit. It was closed, and no one was to pass. That was the way his Master wanted it. The swordsman sighed deeply. He returned his sword to its sheath, and sat down on a big rock outside the gate.[2]

Here we have an obviously powerful warrior confronting a barrier that he can't overcome. He can go no further. No matter what physical or material strength the swordsman applies, he cannot open this gate. Like this swordsman, we, too, will someday face the point in our lives where we can't get to where we want be. The place where the gate is not open to us. And, like this hero, we will have to put our swords away and wait for the forces outside our heroic ego to create the next step.

Seven years earlier on the day he was to leave the mountain, his Master looked at him for a long moment without speaking. There was a kind expression in his eyes and something else, too, something that resembled pity. He could only bow his head in silence when his eyes encountered the compassionate and tolerant eyes of his Master. A while later, the old man said to him, "I cannot keep you at my side forever. Sooner or later, you must go down the mountain and into the world where you will have many opportunities in which to carry out the Way and to help people. I thought that perhaps I could keep you here with me a little longer, but if it's your will to go, my child, then go

---

[2]Thich Nhat Hanh, *The Pine Gate* (Fredonia, NY: White Pine Press, 1988). Used by permission.

in peace. There is only this: Remember, always, what I have taught you and given to you, always. Down in the world below this mountain, you will need all of it."

Then his Master went over briefly again what he was to avoid, seek, leave alone, and change. Finally, he put a gentle hand on his shoulder: "Those are the yardsticks for your actions. Never do anything that could cause suffering either to yourself or to others, in the present or in the future. And go without fear on the road which you believe will lead you and others to total enlightenment. Remember, always, the standards by which happiness and suffering, illusion and liberation must be measured. Without them, you would betray the Way itself, let alone help the world!"

Here we see the teachings of the masters and how they are meant to be lived in the world. Without them we can do more damage than good.

"I have already given you my precious sword. Use it to subdue monsters and devils. But I want you to look upon it more like a sharp blade that comes from your own heart with which you will subjugate your own ambitions and desires. Now, I have this for you, too, and this will make your task easier." Then his Master pulled out of his wide sleeve a small viewing glass, and handed it to him.

"This is the Me Ngo glass," he said. "It will help you to determine good and evil, to separate the virtuous from the wicked. It is also called the Demon Viewer, for looking through it, you will see the true forms of demons, evil spirits, and the like . . ."

He received the fabulous viewing glass from
his Master's hand, but he was so grateful and so
deeply moved he could not say one word. The following day, at the break of dawn, he went up to
the central hall to take leave of his old Master. . . .
The teacher called after his disciple, "Remember,
my child, poverty cannot weaken you, wealth cannot seduce you, power cannot vanquish you. I will
be here for the day you come back, your vows fulfilled!"

He recalled the first days of his journey
vividly. Then, months and years went through his
mind. How humanity had revealed itself to him
under different guises! And how helpful the
sword and the Me Ngo viewing glass had been to
him! Once, he met a priest whose appearance
instantly inspired reverence, who—such an honor
for the young swordsman—invited him back to
his retreat where they would, in the words of the
old sage, "discuss how best to join their efforts for
the purposes of helping their fellow human
beings." At first, the young man listened with
rapture, but then, something odd about the priest
struck him. He whipped out the Me Ngo and
looked through it. In front of him, there was a
gigantic demon! Its blue eyes sent forth crackling
sparks, a horn stood out from its forehead, and its
fangs were as long as his own arms! In one jump,
the young man backed away, drew his sword, and
furiously attacked it. The demon fought back but,
of course, had no chance. It prostrated itself at the
young man's foot, begging for mercy. The swordsman then demanded that it swear, under oath, it
would return where it had come from, to study
the Way, pray that one day it would be permitted
to come back into the world of men as a true
human being, and refrain from ever disguising

itself again as a priest to bewitch and devour the innocent. Another time, he met a mandarin, an old man with a long white beard. It was a happy encounter between a young hero out to save the world and a high official, a "father and mother to the people," bent on finding better and better ways to govern and benefit the masses. Again, the young man's instinct was aroused; under the Me Ngo, the handsome, awe-inspiring old official turned out to be an enormous hog whose eyes literally dripped with greed. In one instant, the sword flew out of its sheath. The hog tried to flee, but the swordsman, in one jump, overtook it. Standing astride the main threshold of the mandarin's mansion, he barred the only escape route. The beast took on its true form and cried out loudly for mercy. Again, the young man did not leave the monster without extracting from it the solemn oath that it would follow the Way, that it would never again take the form of a mandarin so that it could gnaw the flesh and suck the blood of the people.

And there was that time, walking by a marketplace, when he saw a crowd surrounding a bookstall. The picture-and-book seller was a very beautiful young woman whose smile was like an opening flower. Seated nearby was another young woman, also of stunning beauty, who was singing softly some melodious tunes while plucking the strings of a lute. The beauty of the girls and the grace of the songs so captivated everyone present that no one left the stall once they had stopped, and all anyone could do was stand and listen, enraptured, and buy the pictures and books. The young man himself was attracted by the scene. He finally approached and held up one of the pictures. The elegance of the design and vividness of the colors overwhelmed him. Yet, an uneasiness rose within him. He reached for his Me Ngo. The two beautiful girls were actually two enormous snakes whose tongues darted forth and back like knife blades. The swordsman swept everyone aside in one movement of his arms, and with his sword pointing at the monsters, he shouted like thunder, "Demons! Back to your evil nature!"

The crowd scattered in fright. The big snakes swung at the young man, but no sooner did the fabulous sword draw a few flashing circles around their bodies than the reptiles coiled at his feet in submission. He forced their jaws open and carved out their venom-filled fangs with his sword. Then he put the bookstall to the torch and sent the monsters back to their lairs with the solemn promise, against certain total destruction, that they would never come back to bewitch the village people.

So, the young swordsman went on from village to village, and from town to town, on a mission he had set for himself, using the weapon and the viewing glass his Master had given him, along with priceless counsels. He threw himself into his task. For a time now he had come to think of himself as The Indispensable Swordsman.

Here is our first warning of how the hero goes astray. The swordsman originally enters the world carrying the tools of his training. The swordsman, in this story, is a spiritual warrior who desires to help the people in their endless battle of good against evil. In time this hero becomes so involved in the battles, like the twin War Gods of the Hopi myth, that he loses sight of the true situation. Life becomes defined by egoic standards rather than by guidelines taught by the masters and the grandmothers.

172 / MADELINE McMURRAY

And so, seven years passed. One day, as he was resting on the bank of a river, watching the water flow by quietly, he suddenly realized that for some time now he had not used the Me Ngo viewing glass. He had not used it, he was now aware, not because he had forgotten that he had it, but because he had not felt like using it. . . . But, obviously, something odd had happened to him recently, and he did not know what. It seemed to him he began to feel no great joy when he saw wisemen in his viewing glass, just as he felt no great fury when he saw in it the images of monsters and devils. When monsters appeared in his miraculous glass, the young swordsman couldn't help noticing that there happened to be a certain familiarity even in their horrifying inhuman features.

The Me Ngo remained safely in his pocket, even though it had not been used for a long time. Then the young swordsman thought he would return some day to the mountain to ask his Master's advice: why did he have such reluctance to use what obviously had been such a great help to him? But only on the twelfth day of the eighth month, while he was crossing a forest of white plum trees and was struck by the snow-white blossoms gleaming under the autumn moon, did he suddenly yearn for the days when he studied as a young man under his old Master, whose cottage stood at the border of just such an old plum forest. Only then did he decide to return.

Now we see the warrior reaching a point in his life when new questions begin to formulate themselves. The swordsman wondered why he didn't use the Me Ngo glass more fully. He knew the value of the viewing glass and yet he left

it in his pocket. We, too, like the swordsman, come to choice
points in life where new questions present themselves. We
find ourselves asking: "Is this the life I want?" "The life I
thought I'd have?" "How did I end up here?" "Have I used
my gifts?" "My talents?" "Have I done what I set out to
do?" "Is it enough?"

It is the wondering of the hero in this story that opens
him to the possibility of returning to the Master. This same
inner questioning draws each of us toward guidance from
that which is higher; that which is at the top of the mountain. The teacher, guru, shaman, or master is not in the
everyday activity of the world. We must turn (and return)
to that which can teach and guide us. Higher guidance is
often discovered in the silence of inner development.
Deep, personal challenges have a unique way of appear-
ing to us in the privacy of our own rooms or within the
dark hours of sleepless nights. Slowing down our general
patterns of stimulation and overactivity encourages the
discovery of the masters within and around us.

> In his wish to see his Master, the journey back
> seemed interminable: seven days and seven nights
> of climbing hills and crossing streams. But as he
> reached the foot of the high mountain where he
> would begin the ascent to his Master's abode,
> darkness descended. The rising moon showed the
> two leaves of the heavy pine gate shut tightly, pre-
> venting him from going any further up the moun-
> tain.
>
> There was nothing he could do but wait. At
> dawn, he thought, one of his "brothers" would
> certainly come down to fetch water from the
> stream and could open the gate for him. . . . There
> was rustling of dry leaves. The swordsman looked
> up and saw the vague form of someone walking
> down the mountain. He thought it must be one of
> his younger "brothers," though it was not light

enough and the figure was too distant for him to make out the latter's features. It must be a "brother" because the person was carrying something like a large pitcher. Whoever it was came closer and closer, and the swordsman heard him exclaim happily:

—Elder Brother!
—Younger Brother!
—When did you arrive? Just now?
—No! As a matter of fact, I arrived here when the moon was just coming up! I've waited all night down here. Why, in Heaven's name, did anyone lock up the gate like this? Was it the Master's order?

The younger disciple, smiling, raised his hand and pulled, ever so lightly, at the heavy gate. It swung open with ease. . . . The younger brother explains that the Master doesn't want to see anyone unless he has a true determination to learn. . . . the gate will open itself for virtuous people but would stay shut and bar the way for those too heavy with the dust of the world! There is no way anyone could ever climb it or jump over it. Especially someone burdened with the spirits of demons and the like! The swordsman knitted his brows:

—Would you say I am such a person? Would you? Why did the gate stay shut for me?

The younger man laughed heartily:

—But of course not! How could you be such a person? Anyway, we can go up now, you see that the way is clear. But just a moment, Elder Brother! I must fetch some water first. Come with me. Smile, Brother, smile! Who are you angry at?

. . . The water was tinted a pale rose by the dawn. There, they could see their reflections next to one another. The swordsman was bold and strong in his knight's suit; a long sword slung diagonally over his back. The younger disciple's figure was gentler in his flowing page's robe, a pitcher in his hands. Without speaking, both looked at their own reflections and smiled at one another. A water-spider sprung up suddenly and caused the rose-tinted surface to ripple, sending the images into thousands of undulating patterns.

. . . The younger brother asked; "Do you still have the Me Ngo viewing glass with you? Master gave it to you when you came down the mountains years ago!"

The swordsman realized that it was true, that all these years he had used it only to look at others but never once had he looked at his own image. He took the glass out, wiped it on his sleeve, then pointed it at the water's surface. The two heads came close to look through the small glass together.

A loud scream escaped from the throat of the two young men. It reverberated through the forest. The swordsman fell forward and collapsed on the bank of the stream. A deer, drinking water further upstream, looked up in fright.

The younger disciple could not believe what he had seen in the glass; there he was in his flowing robe, a pitcher in hand, standing next to a towering demon with eyes deep and dark like waterwells and long fangs curving down around his square jaw. Yes, he saw the color of the demon's face. It was a bluish gray, the shade of ashes and death. The young man shuddered, and rubbing his eyes, looked again at his senior who was now lying unconscious on the blue stones of the bank. The older man's face still expressed shock and horror; suffering had been etched upon this man who, for seven years, had ceaselessly braved the rough and cruel world down below their mountain retreat.

The young disciple rushed down to the stream to fetch water and to douse his elder's face with it. Moments later, the swordsman came to. His face was ravaged with despair. His true image had appeared in the Me Ngo so unexpectedly, bringing self-knowledge to him in such a swift, brutal fashion that he could do nothing but collapse under this blow. All his energy seemed to have left him. He tried to stand up, but there was no strength in his legs and arms.

—It's all right, it's all right, my brother! We'll go up now.

To the swordsman's ears, his brother's voice was like an imperceptible movement of the breeze, a faint murmur from afar. He shook his head. His world had collapsed, and he wanted to live no longer! He felt as if his body and soul had been in the path of a hurricane. He could not possibly entertain the idea, the affront, of bringing himself, ever, into his beloved Master's presence.

The Younger man brushed some sand off his brother's shoulder:

—No, you shouldn't worry about it. You know that the Master had nothing but compassion for you. Let's go up now. We'll again live and work and study together . . .

Before the swordsman reaches the Master, before he moves through the gate to ascend the mountain, there is a long exchange with the younger monk. This is the kind of dialogue that goes on within the psyche as we try to find our way back to the Master; the dialogue of questioning that leads to truth. When the younger brother explains why the gate won't open, the swordsman wonders if he could be one of those to whom it is locked. As the two look into the mirror of the water, the younger man asks if the swordsman still uses the viewing glass. These questions reconnect the heroic ego to deeper self-examination.

In this story, the Master is the ancient knowledge that is available to those who seek it. The Master, like the Spider Grandmother, is a reminder of the healing possibility for the hero. The healing in this myth comes in the form of compassion. Once the Swordsman sees his own image clearly, he knows how far he has roamed from the Master's teachings. The younger brother is the reminder that compassion sees clearly and desires healing. This is the gift of the Master in this story and of Spider Grandmother in the Hopi story.

In the first story, Spider Grandmother intervenes through her medicine. In the second story, the Master waits beyond the pine gate for the swordsman's return. The two myths are similar in that they show us the warrior's ongoing relationship to a wiser influence. Two stories: one Hopi, one Buddhist, one ancient, one modern. Both revealing their mythic understanding of the hero's development to another stage, a stage that is guided by wisdom and compassion.

The wisdom figures of the Master and Spider Grandmother provide yet another option in our mythic choices. Powerful and complex energies are contained in these figures. They are images for the wisdom of the ages—the knowledge of life and fate, the creator, protector and healer. Where is this wisdom and healing in our world today? How can we retrieve the lost mythology of protectors and guides moving in our lives?

Biblical tradition teaches us that fear of the Lord is the beginning of wisdom. Sacred consciousness begins with respect and regard for eternal wisdom. If the hero is ego, then the master/grandmother is soul—a wisdom of soul that connects to the eternal principles of life and guides the individual beyond heroic consciousness. In psychological terms, the master/grandmother are archetypal models for mature development.

We can choose to work toward wisdom, or we can continue to ignore her. Wisdom is not lost, just lonely. "The Wisdom of Solomon" makes wisdom's availability apparent:

> Wisdom shines bright and never fades; she is easily discerned by those who love her, and by those who seek her she is found. She is quick to make herself known to those who desire knowledge of her; the man who rises early in search of her will not grow weary in the quest, for he will find her seated at his door. To set all one's thoughts on her is prudence in its perfect shape, and to lie wakeful in her cause is the short way to peace of mind. For she herself ranges in search of those who are worthy of her; on their daily path she appears to them with kindly intent, and in all their purposes meets them half-way.[3]

In Ecclesiasticus, Wisdom is the first of all created things. She is the intelligent purpose who participated with the Lord in the creation of the world. The Lord God is so vast, so awe-inspiring, so powerful, so almighty that the human cannot gaze upon His face and live. It is the feminine co-creator of biblical mythology, presented in wisdom litera-

---

[3]"The Wisdom of Solomon," 6:12–17, The New English Bible (New York: Cambridge University Press, 1971).

ture, who is personal, knowable and available. The creative feminine principle is a pattern within us that can be brought into the activities of daily life.

Battles of power and dominance must be given up in favor of the development of human qualities which connect to wisdom. Again, Ecclesiasticus tells us that if we desire wisdom we need to do the following: control the emotion of anger, keep the commandments of the Lord, be disciplined in our behaviors, be sure to speak true, never be arrogant, develop humility, and love God and try to do his will. In Buddhism there are meditative practices designed to guide the seeker toward understanding of the five wisdoms. In this tradition, the necessary attitudes for acquiring wisdom are compassion, love, rejoicing in the good fortune of others, and equanimity. Wisdom is viewed as attainable awareness.

THE LOSS OF WISDOM

In the college classroom I ask students to list the mythic values given to them through family and community. They always bring up the ideals of loving one's neighbor, living by the Ten Commandments, and freedom and justice for all. When I go the next step and ask them to apply these ideals to the actual events of human life, such as relationships, economics, politics, policy-making, and law enforcement they begin to go blank. It is not possible, they tell me, to use the myths of the Western collective in the reality of specific situations. These young people reflect to me the death of wisdom and an attitude that considers the Master and Grandmother Spider as fantasy figures designed to entertain children.

The consequence of losing the teachings of the ancient ones is that when values and ethics are left to the unconscious side of personality, they eventually reemerge into consciousness as fanaticism. Basic mythic structures don't go away. They either become part of an open and changing system, or they go in the direction of closed and rigid ideations. We can check ourselves: when our approach to life is the only "right" approach, the psyche is not an open system. When self-righteous, hero-conqueror consciousness forces itself into every corner of the nation at the expense of anyone or anything that dares to question its authority, wisdom and compassion are lost, and society lies in the darker side of heroic power.

When kings kill culture's children—whether it be in the mythology of Herod killing Bethlehem's newly born, or the massacre of the students in Tiananmen Square in modern China—we know wisdom has been squeezed out by unbridled power. Without the human qualities of compassion and wisdom we ignore real situations that don't fit our one-sided position. I may profess to love my neighbor, but if I can't understand "neighbor" beyond my own culture, I am not wise. I may think that I believe in life, liberty, and the pursuit of happiness, but if these ideals are only available as I define them, I am not wise. If I am one-sided, rigid, and dogmatic the work of growing-my-soul is left undone.

Mythic teachings give us constructs for living that can be brought into the light of day for conscious evaluation. Wisdom and compassion are human behaviors that we can choose to develop. Qualities of love, truth, humility, and compassion are real and can be put into practice. One does not have to spend years in psychotherapy, or retreat to some mountaintop to break heroic patterns. The willingness to be self-reflective and the honesty to face what one sees are primary requirements that lie within our capacity. For example, if I am a person who loses my temper, I must see that "I" lose my temper and stop blaming others for "making me" do it. Honesty in seeing can begin to change everything. We must openly question behaviors and evaluate them in terms of the teachings of wisdom.

Lived consciously, these mythic constructs of honesty, kindness, love, and compassion are psychological stances that produce wise people open to the movements of life. The ability to be self-reflective does not put us above the rest of creation, but it does enable us to understand our relationship to the greater whole of creation.

EXERCISE 12

WISDOM'S INTERVENTIONS

We tend to think that we do everything ourselves. In fact, life is usually more complex than we acknowledge. The wisdom of the master/grandmother is more active in our lives than we acknowledge. Spider Grandmother knew what the warrior twins would need before they needed it; she gave them medicine and told them to take their bows and arrows when they went out. The Master knew what tools the swordsman would need in the world, as well as offering assurance that he would be available when the swordsman returned. Both wisdom figures, in these two separate stories, are participating in the lives of the heroes even when their presence is not obvious. To become more aware of the mythic dimension operating in your own life take time to do the following:

1. Make a list of the important events of your life, i.e., accomplishments, people you've met, choices you've made, places you've been.

2. Next to each item on your list note the original spark that turned you in that direction.

3. Dare to be impressed by the lack of control on your part and the wisdom of the interventions of the larger patterns.

Note: Ordinary events change our lives. Let me share an example: when I first became interested in Jungian psychology, I attended a seminar led by an analyst from Los Angeles. I live far north and asked him how I might go about getting more connected to this particular psychology. He referred me to a group I'd never heard of. I took his advice because I had enjoyed my weekend. I trusted a complete stranger. I then spent the next eight years of my life working and training with the group he had sent me to. When I look back, I realize that this person could have sent me anywhere. I sense now that some larger wisdom was guiding my life at a time when it needed direction. One person, one moment in time, and my life was changed. I often wonder at the mystery of it all. What if I had gone to a different seminar with a different leader? What other path might I have walked?

CHAPTER ELEVEN

THE WISDOM
OF SACRIFICE

Finding wisdom and compassion in the inner reaches of our being, and bringing those discoveries into conscious living, are aspects of the mythology of individuation. C. G. Jung provides us with a theoretical framework for the psychological processes of adult development. More importantly, he gives us a living model through the sharing of his own life experiences. In regard to heroic consciousness, C. G. Jung said:

> . . . identity and my heroic idealism had to be abandoned, for there are higher things than the ego's will, and to these one must bow.[1]

To admit that we must give up our well-developed identities and follow something other than our ego's will seems almost too much for most of us to bear. Instead, we prefer egoic psychologies that tell us we can "have it all" and do what we will. We prefer messages that tell us we only have to keep our minds on a positive track to avoid all suffering. The possibility that adult development includes the ego following deeper demands is something that we have yet to explore.

Sacrifice is actually elemental to both Eastern and Western mythology. In Christianity, for example, the Christ figure is sacrificed for the sins of the world. In Buddhism, the enlightened one, the Bodhisattva, foregoes entering Nir-

---

[1] C. G. Jung, *Memories, Dreams, Reflections*, Aniela Jaffé, ed. (New York: Random House, 1965), pp. 180–181.

vana to help others. The mystery cults of Persia professed that the god of light, Mithra, was sacrificed to engender the world and its vegetation. In ancient Egyptian mythology the eternally good being, Osiris, was murdered by his brother only to become the judge in the realm of the dead, as well as the one who generates plant life on the surface of the Earth. In shamanic traditions around the world, the shaman dies in order to attain knowledge of the immortals and is then reborn to bring this knowledge to the people.

Sacrifice is the primary pattern of death-rebirth covered in an earlier section. I return to it here as a reminder of its importance to human development. Moving through the stages of our lives, we experience the motif of sacrifice time and time again. Making our next step always means leaving our present level of development behind us. This is easily illustrated on the physical plane. We are in fact physically different at age 2, 13, 29, 50, and so on. We are also emotionally and spiritually different at each age of our lives. We can't stop the physical process of growing older. Unfortunately, we can stop our emotional and spiritual development through the unwillingness to sacrifice our present modes of behavior for the possibilities of future becoming. The new cannot be born until the old has passed away.

On the path of becoming our own specific persons, the myth of sacrifice is a theme that helps us experience meaning in the act of following an authority greater than either our personal definitions or our collective indoctrination. The sacrifice of our ego-as-final-authority is more difficult than the natural sacrifices that we all make in our lives. Parents sacrifice their own needs to meet the needs of their children, or individuals sacrifice the desires of the moment for a larger goal in the future. Although these sacrifices serve the continuity of family and community, there is still another level of sacrifice that is made in later life development. Ego-as-center must be let go of for soul to blossom. When ego yearns for soul, life's situations and the human psyche intertwine for new creation.

Jung followed the guidance that came to him in dreams and imagination. A primary inner personality for Jung was the image of the wise old man. Jung called this figure Philemon (figure 13, page 186). He gives the following description of Philemon:

> Philemon and other figures of my fantasies brought home to me the crucial insight that there are things in the psyche which I do not produce, but which produce themselves and have their own life. Philemon represented a force which was not myself. In my fantasies I held conversations with him, and he said things which I had not consciously thought. For I observed clearly that it was he who spoke, not I. He said I treated thoughts as if I generated them myself, but in his view thoughts were like animals in the forest, or people in a room, or birds in the air, and added, "If you should see people in a room, you would not think that you had made those people, or that you were responsible for them." It was he who taught me psychic objectivity, the reality of the psyche. Through him the distinction was clarified between myself and the object of my thought. He confronted me in an objective manner, and I understood that there is something in me which can say things that I do not know and do not intend, things which may even be directed against me.
>
> Psychologically, Philemon represented superior insight. He was a mysterious figure to me. At times he seemed to me quite real, as if he were a living personality. I went walking up and down the garden with him, and to me he was what the Indians call a guru.[2]

---

[2]*Memories, Dreams, Reflections*, p. 183.

Figure 13. "Philemon," the figure to whom C. G. Jung attributed higher insight. Jung came to know this image as a guiding force for the formation of much of his psychological perspective. Painting by C. G. Jung in the Red Book. Illustration copyright © the estate of C. G. Jung. Used by permission.

Philemon first appeared in a dream. Jung painted a detailed picture of this winged figure so that he would not forget him. We, like Jung, are required to discover the interface of conscious and unconscious by remembering our dreams and images. Without remembering, superior insight remains forever unconscious. We learn through being in relationship to what is presented by the archetypal psyche. C. G. Jung experienced Philemon as guide into the structure of personality. The consciousness acquired through this figure moved Jung beyond previous theories into relationship with the collective/archetypal unconscious.

Jung realized that the model of the heroic ego, although dominant for the culture, was not his myth. He was brought to the realization that sacrifice of the ego position was necessary. To be true to his own experiences of the archetypal psyche, his life's work had to circumambulate the exploration of Philemon's superior insight. Jung saw the symbol of the mandala as an image for the non-personal Self at the center of the psyche. He connected of the mythic structures of the collective unconscious to a transpersonal center of consciousness that gives meaning and purpose to life. Jung said of these understandings:

> Such things cannot be thought up but must grow again from the forgotten depths if they are to express the supreme insights of consciousness and the loftiest intuitions of the spirit, and in this way fuse the uniqueness of present-day consciousness with the age-old past of life.... "When I began drawing the mandalas ... I saw that everything, all the paths I had been following, all the steps I had taken, were leading back to a single point— namely, to the mid-point. It became increasingly plain to me that the mandala is the center. It is the

exponent of all paths. It is the path to the center, to individuation."[3]

The challenge to Jung—to accept that his thoughts were not his own and that there were ideas that belonged to the non-personal dimension moving through him—is also our challenge today. Because of his experiences of the mythic dimension, Jung lived a life filled with suffering as well as success. He did not take the easier path of being Freud's successor. He had to sacrifice his position as favored student to be reborn into his specific destiny. His path was to explore the inner labyrinth of the human psyche to find wisdom at its center. By shouldering this personal journey, Jung made major contributions to the fields of both psychology and religion, contributions that came directly out of his relationship to, and experience of, the archetypal psyche. We, too, are called to discover our own relatedness to soul that holds a wider and deeper understanding of life.

The pre-Columbian Kogi, with the wisdom of the Elder Brothers, have an intimate understanding of how life on Earth works. We, living in what we call the age of information, are unable to grasp the relationship between ourselves and the world around us. We "know" that the oxygen cycle includes plant life, we "know" the rate at which we eat up the forests, but we do not "know" that our misuse of the forests is contributing to the destruction of the quality of life on this planet. We know that the ozone layer is breaking down, we know the rate at which we put destructive chemicals into the air, but we do not "know" that we are killing life through over-exposure to the rays of the Sun. If our knowing-knowledge were at a deeper level, we would have to take information seriously and change our behaviors. We prefer to stay asleep in our ego unconsciousness, no matter what the price.

---

[3]Aniela Jaffé, ed., *C. G. Jung: Word and Image*, Bollingen Series CVII, 2 (Princeton, NJ: Princeton University Press, 1979), pp. 77–78.

Einstein's words, "Since the splitting of the atom everything has changed except our way of thinking,"[4] are unnervingly accurate. We have yet to wake up to what we know. We must challenge ourselves to a broader range of development. In the Japanese fairy tale, "The Sparrow's Gift," the sparrow offers an old man two boxes, one large and one small, as a gift to repay his kindness. The old man, being gracious, takes the small one. When he returns home the box contains gold coins. When the old man's wife, who has always been mean to the sparrow, learns that there is still a larger box at the sparrow's house, she goes to the sparrow, and out of greed, says she will retrieve the box for her husband. When the old woman opens the large box, it turns out to be filled, not with gold coins, but with monsters. She runs to her husband and hides behind him until the demons finally return to the forest. The story tells us:

> . . . . that from that day on the old woman became kinder and more gracious. And so she and her husband lived in happiness for the rest of their days, treasuring their gifts from the sparrow fairy—gold from the small box, and wisdom from the large.[5]

Stories of wisdom teach us of her availability if we choose to pay the price. Wisdom is the pearl of great price, but the cost is not dollars and cents. The price paid is the sacrifice of one-sided development. Like the old woman, we must sacrifice greed, power, cruelty—all those patterns of behavior that keep us from appreciating life's gifts.

Through following the mythic aspect of personality, we wake up to the world around us. Wisdom speaks for the

---

[4]Albert Einstein, from a telegram of the Emergency Committee of Atomic Scientists, over Einstein's signature. Quoted in O. Nathan and H. Norden, *Einstein on Peace* (New York: Avenel Books, 1960), p. 376.
[5]Allan B. Chinen, "The Sparrow's Gift," from *In the Ever After* (Wilmette, IL: Chiron Publications, 1989), pp. 17–20.

whole system. In order to hear her we must extend ourselves into her perspective. We cannot own wisdom as a
personal commodity, or expect her to fit our demands and
expectations. Wisdom belongs to the world. Your wisdom is
not more important than my wisdom. Wisdom is not a club
we join. Wisdom is not a system of dogmas or beliefs. Wisdom does not make us special or more unique. Wisdom
wakes us up! Wisdom is the gift of the soul.

Psyche presents herself—the choice to receive and
respond is ours to make over and over again. Soul development surrounds us in the activities of both waking and
sleeping. Small things as well as large formulate our becoming. Life is forever creating itself. I wake in the morning
with a dream about Spider Woman. I want to create an
image of her to help me hold the energy of the dream. I look
through a book on southwestern mythology to stimulate
my imagination. I spot a design I feel to be "just right." I
spend time creating my own image. When I finish drawing,
I decide to take a moment to read the text that refers to this
image. It so happens that it is the story of the twin War
Gods and Spider Grandmother. I realize that this story
wants to become part of this book.

As I listen to what is presented and respond to it, I
experience psyche moving in the activity of my life. The
anima mundi, the soul of the world that interacts with my
soul and is the essence of my soul, offers me an opportunity to participate in that which is unfolding within and
around me. If I ignore the image of Spider Woman in my
dream, I miss the story that is waiting to become part of
my life.

The most valuable, and still neglected, connection to the
mythic psyche is the wisdom of the dream. It is in sleep that
the ego is finally set aside. Modern consciousness discon-
nects itself from expansion by being unwilling to carry
dreams into conscious living. In the mythic tradition of the
Talmud, it is said that a dream that is not interpreted is like a
letter that is not read. God sends letters of prophecy to the

community through "visions of the night."[6] In classical
Greek tradition it was the dream that was central to the healing rituals held in the sanctuary of the god Asclepius. In
India, the birth of the prophet Mahavira, the twenty-fourth
prophet of Jainism, was foretold to Queen Trisala in a dream.
And in Christian myth, Joseph was warned in a dream of
the dangers to the life of the Christ Child, and was told to
take the Holy Mother and her son into the land of Egypt.

Like Joseph, we must follow the visions of the night
and embrace the dream's message as though an angel had
whispered in our ear. Dreams must be met as they are presented and the ego cannot be allowed to change or manipulate them. The voice of soul comes in the night as guiding
wisdom—sometimes personal, sometimes archetypal, but if
listened to, always helpful. It can provide a correction of an
earlier perception, a reflection of an attitude we hadn't considered, a statement about relationship, a glimpse into the
future, an insight into life here on Earth, a mythic statement
connecting us more fully to our collective. Any and all of
these possibilities are contained in the material of the dream
world.

The following two dreams illustrate how the psyche
offers personal and mythic development when the dreamer
(dream-ego) willingly participates.

> The first dream is of three men descending a stair-
> case into a cellar. The dreamer is a woman and
> she is watching the three men. As they reach the
> bottom of the cellar the dreamer realized that they
> are in the crypt of Mary, the Holy Mother. One of
> the men, a very dashing character, walks up to the
> casket to look at the wood carving of Mary. As he
> gazes at her he places his hands on the casket. At
> this point the dreamer can see through the carv-
> ing of Mary, into the interior of the casket, where

---

[6]Joel Covitz, *Visions of the Night* (Boston: Shambhala, 1990).

she sees the body of the Holy Mother. She sees that the hands of the Virgin are beginning to have a golden glow around them. The dreamer sees that the Holy Mother is beginning to extend her hands through the top of the casket to touch the hands of the young man. As her hands move, her body comes to life. Mary, the Holy Mother, sits up and is a living figure. The three men and the dreamer are filled with awe and amazement at what is happening.[7]

The dreamer awakes with the realization that the Divine Mother is becoming active in her. She also knows that this is a dream of future development. The dream work is hers to complete. She will have to make the descent into herself that will bring her to the dark crypt of the Holy Feminine. A personal embracing of the Holy Mother is possible within this dream. There is also the awakening of the sacred feminine in the world around us. Goddess mythology is being enlivened, not only in this individual dreamer, but in dreamers, teachers, and women's seminars throughout Western culture. We must sacrifice our old understandings of the god and remythologize the divine to include the goddess. She awakes as a living mythic possibility for each of us.

The second dream comes from a male client who dreamed that he and his wife entered a monastery:

The dreamer's wife is handed a brown paper bag as they go through the doorway of the monastery. When she opens the bag she sees that it is filled with what seem to be pieces of a puzzle. She is a bit disappointed about this. She had expected something more important to be in this bag. Now the wife takes the puzzle pieces from the bag and

---

[7]These dreams are from two clients. Used by permission.

places them carelessly on the table. Instantly, the
dreamer sees that these pieces can be put together
to form the head of Christ.

In waking and remembering the dream, the dreamer
becomes aware of the divine center that is waiting to be
explored in the depths of his own being. The two dreams
share a common wisdom of sacred activity within personality as well as within the world. The image of Christ, like the
image of the Holy Mother, is being revisioned in the world
of theology. Christ-centeredness and Christ-consciousness
hold possibilities of inclusiveness that are yet to be developed in our modern world.

The images of these dreams are expressions of the religious nature of the deep psyche. They are sacred images
that are only as far away from us as we insist on keeping
them. Although we may not dream of the Holy Mother or
the Christ, there are endless images and experiences that
express this same wisdom. If trees and rivers come alive to
us, or animals speak in dreams, we, too, are touching the
depths of psyche's images. When dreams present puzzles to
be put together, or riddles to be solved, we, too, are working in the land of sacred challenges.

Dreams, as important as they are, are not the only
entrance into sacred awareness. Pathways into mature
development and the consciousness of wisdom surround us.
There are paths within religious traditions, spiritual disci-
plines, meditation, prayer, visualization, ritual, active imagination, creativity, and relationship with nature, to name a
few. The mythic dimension permeates existence. It is the
invisible world behind the visible world. Myth is within us,
in the depth of the soul. And myth is around us, in expressions of the soul. Art, music, theater, social actions, collective
movements, religious practices, and political systems are all
reflections of the archetypal psyche. The masks of the gods
and goddesses present themselves in an endless and varied
procession moving within the matrix of creation.

CHAPTER TWELVE

TOWARD
A NEW MYTHOLOGY

Our present development, individual and collective, requires movement toward a psycho-spiritual position of wisdom. Mythologies of the sage, the wise old man and the grandmothers are much neglected in the modern world.

Each day, as I watch and listen to the national news, I see the hero out of control. Some days it's a big story, like the Rodney King case, or the most recent terrorist attack. Other days it's straightforward one-liners telling me that last year 37,000 Americans died violently in our streets. I hear regularly about guns and teenagers and am horrified to hear reports of children killing children. I can't help but see the violent behavior of our citizenship as partially due to the over-glorification of the heroic image. A quick glance at movie posters, video games, and the options available on satellite television tells me that we are trying to be something that we can't always be. We want to be biggest, best, on top, most powerful, dominant, rich, beautiful, strong, thin, glamorous, etc. etc. We have no room for ordinary living.

How much longer can we stay in these heroic cycles of win or lose? Where are the words, the actions, the knowledge that will lead to a better quality of life? For the planet? For her citizens? This call for a new mythology is neither idealism nor romanticism. The mythology of the conquering hero, as a primary worldview, is no longer viable.

In being attentive to the depths of mythic consciousness we can access the unknown development that lies before us. We cannot know ahead of time what the future holds, but clearly, we are meant to grow up. Hopefully the message of our Elder Brothers, the Kogi, is correct: "The world does not have to end. If we act well the world can go on." To discover what is required to "act well" we will first have to stop conquering and start listening; stop competing and start caring; stop dominating and start learning.

The eightfold path of Buddhism reminds us that we need right view, right resolve, right speech, right conduct, right livelihood, right effort, right mindfulness, and right concentration. Each of these is a way of acting well, "that the world does not have to end." Chief Seattle, of the Suquamish tribe, tells us that we must teach our children that the Earth is sacred. "That the Earth is our mother. Whatever befalls the Earth befalls the sons of the earth. If men spit upon the ground they spit upon themselves."[1] Like Buddhism, native traditions show us what it means to "act well" that the earth can go on. Teachings about living myths for future becoming surround us. We must walk through their thresholds.

In a series of 12th-century drawings called the Oxherding Pictures, the Chinese master Kakuan illustrated the steps of awareness that lead to enlightenment. In the first picture, we see a childlike figure searching for the eternal principle of life. In the tenth picture we find a grown man who has found his place in the world as an ordinary being who helps others. The text that goes with this last drawing reads:

> Barefooted and naked of breast, I mingle with the people of the world.
> My clothes are ragged and dust-laden, and I am ever blissful.
> I use no magic to extend my life;
> Now, before me, the dead trees become alive.[2]

---

[1]Chief Seattle delivered a speech in 1851 called "This Earth is Sacred to my People," reproduced by the Northcoast Environmental Center, Arcata, CA.
[2]Paul Reps, ed. *Zen Flesh, Zen Bones* (Boston, Rutland, Tokyo: Charles E. Tuttle, 1957), p. 186.

Figure 14. The sage, or wisdom figure, from the Oxherding Pictures, reveals a relatedness between student and teacher—the continuity of generations. Illustration for *Zen Flesh, Zen Bones*, compiled by Paul Reps (Boston, Rutland, Tokyo: Charles E. Tuttle, 1957). Copyright Charles E. Tuttle. Used by permission.

This passage describes an ordinary / non-ordinary person. One who uses no magic and yet brings life where there is death. In this oriental model, we find a person who has attained an awareness of the deep source of all life. He is always blissful, even when his outer situation is a bit ragged. What psychological development is this? Do we know anything about being in the world this way? The qualities of the

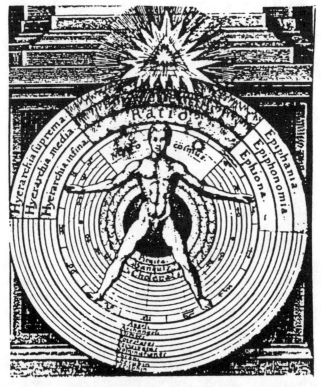

Figure 15. The individual as the "center" is deeply in-grained in Western tradition. We are challenged to bring this image to a more mature development, that the inclusiveness of life might become more available to human insight. From the title page of Robert Fludd's *Utriusque cosmi . . . historia,* 1617–1619.

sage are expressed in an ability to embrace opposites; moving beyond duality while knowing the double nature of life. As the zen master might say, "Not two and not one." Healing stands next to being without magic; while ragged and dust-laden are connected to being ever blissful. Wisdom transcends opposites, finding relatedness through paradox. The sage acquires experience of the animating source behind all life and moves into the world with knowledge of the eternal. In this wise figure we have a mythology that can transform the adolescent egoic stance of our present development into a healthier position for future living.

To contrast the image of the sage portrayed in the Oxherding Pictures with the Renaissance images of our relation to the universe (also an image for enlightenment) reveals our collective situation. The Eastern image shows the wisdom figure relating to a younger person, the mythology of teacher relating to student. The Western image depicts one person in relation to the rest of the universe, the mythology of the individual. Today, we must move toward a more inclusive mythology of integrating the individual into his or her community and redefining community as the whole of creation. It is also interesting that the Sage in the Oxherding Pictures is an old man, while the person in the Renaissance image is much younger. Not a child, but not an adult. This is where we are today, no longer children and not yet wise.

Wisdom requires a collective mythology that can tolerate difference, value diversity, live with pluralism, think in whole systems, integrate the problem of evil, and understand our relatedness and interdependence with everyone and everything in creation. This more inclusive consciousness is not an easy or comfortable development, but is essential to the future of our species. The mythic movement of our age changes who we are and how we act.

We change more than we realize. What once seemed impossible, or unheard of, becomes the norm. The uncreated comes into being. We can either block the movement of soul or participate with her. We must learn that participation is not control. Participation is action, reaction, exchange, dialogue, interaction, and response. To participate is to have a share in the whole, as contrasted to trying to be the whole. We are players in the game of life, not life's creator or director. To think that we create the future is simply a modern way of trying to keep the ego in the driver's seat. We have yet to push egoic human-centeredness aside and encourage mythologies of human participation.

A mythology of participation with the divine is seen in the story of Moses and the burning bush from the Hebrew scriptures. The story begins with Moses tending his flock near Horeb, the mountain of God. This is an important beginning—the daily activity is in a sacred place.

> There the angel of the Lord appeared to him in the flame of a burning bush. Moses noticed that, although the bush was on fire, it was not being burnt up; so he said to himself, "I must go across to see this wonderful sight. Why does not the bush burn away?" When the Lord saw that Moses had turned aside to look, he called to him out of the bush. "Moses, Moses." And Moses answered, "Yes, I am here." God said, "Come no nearer; take off your sandals; the place where you are standing is holy ground. I am the God of your forefathers, the God of Abraham, the God of Isaac, the God of Jacob." Moses covered his face, for he was afraid to gaze on God.[3]

The dialogic nature of this story provides a model for divine-human participation. In the wilderness, Moses sees an image of god that is powerful enough to draw him away from his daily task of tending his flock. We, like Moses, must turn aside when something of the divine appears.

---

[3]Exodus 3:2–6; 4:21–25. New English Bible.

Had Moses passed the bush of flame there would be no story. Only when he explores, wonders, and responds does the sacred call his name. We, too, must dare to be stopped by the appearance of the divine along our path. In attentiveness to life's presentations we encounter dynamic intimacy with the sacred activity of life. The myth of Moses and the burning bush reminds us that response to the presentational-divine leads to an inclusive awareness of the sacred around us. We, too, are standing on holy ground.

In this relationship between the Lord and Moses there is a long interaction in which this god wants something of this person, a dialogue in which the sacred comes into specific form. The Lord wants Moses to go into Egypt and talk Pharaoh into freeing the Israelites. Moses, just like the rest of us, has some pretty good reasons why he can't do what God desires. First of all, he is certain that Pharaoh won't believe that God has sent him. Secondly, he reminds God that he, Moses, isn't a very good speaker. Moses even suggests that it might be better if God were to send someone else.

In this myth we see that the divine makes demands, demands that require change, changes that come through seeing, listening, and responding in daily life. These changes also require that we be guided by something more than our personal position. Like Moses, we will struggle with what is asked of us. And, like Moses, we will acquire a new knowledge of our relationship to the rest of creation. Other changes, changes in understanding, come later in the story. God sends Moses into Egypt while telling him to keep in mind that God will make Pharaoh "obstinate and he will not let the people go." A few lines later we read that "During the journey, while they were encamped for the night, the Lord met Moses, meaning to kill him . . ." Like Moses, we must change our understanding of the divinity by learning to include the opposite natures of the gods and goddesses. We must face a divinity who protects as well as threatens, helps as well as makes difficult, creates as well as destroys. This complex divinity, not Moses, is in charge. Moses completes the task while God directs the action.

Once we know that we are part of the creation of mythology, but not the creator, we may be more able to avoid ego-inflation while doing what is required. Mythologies for the future are emerging from the world unconscious. Participation in these myths will help formulate a new post-heroic consciousness for the next century. The renewed interest in goddess mythology and the archetype of the green man are forms of consciousness that move beyond heroics. Green politics, quantum theory, ecofeminism, Gaia consciousness, and deep ecology (to name a few) are mythic stances that are not anthropocentric. Mythologies of the one-sided power dominance of the hero-warrior-king have yet to give way to mythologies of healing, transformation, sacred living, inclusiveness, co-creation, compassion and wisdom.

Living in this time of mythic transition, we can find our own clarity regarding the myths that surround us. After exploring our personal and collective relationships to the mythology of the hero we expand into the vast mythological world that opens into future becoming. The psychologist William James provides further illumination for our journey into living myths. In *The Varieties of Religious Experience,* James tells us that there are measurable outcomes that can be seen in a religious personality. These same outcomes are applicable to the mythic personality willing to reach into the depth of soul implicit in this book. Development of a personality that has grown in wisdom will include: (1) an awareness of a more spiritual universe that gives meaning and significance to our present reality; (2) spiritual practices that connect the individual to this higher reality and in turn produce effects, psychological and material, in the phenomenal world; (3) an enthusiasm and zest for life, and (4) a personality that reflects self-assurance, a temperament of peace, and an attitude of loving affection toward others.[4]

These guidelines can be used to measure the effectiveness of any mythic position. Without outcomes of a larger perspective, a practice that keeps that perspective growing, and a basic love of the complexity of life, we are more than likely on the wrong track. We must demand that myths for the future meet these basic requirements. Meaning comes from relationship to a spiritual principle that produces real effects in the material world. Myths that support and encourage a living relationship to the eternal in the world are myths worth following into tomorrow. In the end we must be pragmatic when it comes to living myths. Like religious experience, the myths we live are only as valuable as the behaviors that they engender. Mythologies that support a deepening understanding of the sacred and strengthen the human qualities of tolerance, compassion, inclusive-love, and an enchantment with life on Earth are mythologies that we have yet to fully develop.

In the end we may be like Moses, dying outside the promised land. As modern mythmakers, we are asked to give up our ideas of some perfect system that is going to make everything work. Instead, we must grow in openness to that which desires becoming. We cannot determine ahead of time what new forms our world will take. We have only the capacity to be the co-creators of myths. The myths that will guide the future of our species are evolving themselves through us. Whether we will see a coherent mythic structure establish itself in our lifetime I would not dare to predict. Nonetheless, we have a divine destiny to fulfill in freeing ourselves from the dominance of heroics. The future calls for something more.

---

[4]William James, *Varieties of Religious Experience* (New York: Macmillan, 1961), p. 377.

GLOSSARY

Active imagination: Engaging in a dialogue, through words or images, with the figures in dreams; with parts of the unconscious that present themselves; or with information presented in fantasy or visions.

Amplification: Expansion of material from the unconscious through association, active imagination, art or writing.

Archetypes: The deepest level of psychic functioning. Patterns of life that are universally valid. They form the basic content of religions, mythologies, legends and fairytales.

Collective Unconscious: The storehouse of the archetypes. The non-personal realm of personality that is personified through words, images and symbols. Collective unconscious, objective psyche and archetypal psyche are used in this book interchangeably.

Ego: The center of one's consciousness. That part we call "I." A subjective aspect of personality that can choose to relate or not to relate to the collective unconscious. True self, or self with a lower case "s" when used in this book, are also references to ego.

Ego-Self Axis: The vital interrelationship between the ego, as a personal self, and the more than personal, or transpersonal, Self.

Individuation: Expansion of personality to include the total personality—conscious and unconscious. There is also a greater capacity to include the world around us.

Inflation: An emotional state in which one has unrealistically high or low (negative inflation) sense of identity.

Objective Psyche: See collective unconscious.

Personification: The bringing of archetypal energies into images and forms. To personalize the collective unconscious and endow the archetypes with personal intent.

Primordial: A reference to that part of the archetypal psyche that contains the instinctive, the primitive, and the ancient memory of the collective unconscious.

Process: In this book, process is used as a reference to the psychological work of individuation.

Psyche: A feminine dimension of personality, in both men and women, working for relationship to transpersonal development. Psyche and soul are used interchangeably.

Self: An aspect of personality that emerges out of the collective unconscious as a grounding principle for both the ego and the unconscious. An eternal principle available to conscious development. An animating matrix energizing to both the personal and archetypal realms of development. In religious thinking, the Self is similar to the Hindu idea of Brahman as the source of universal life. In Jungian thought, the individuating personality can experience this religious energy at the depths of being.

Soul: Contains the faculty of relatedness to the gods and goddesses. Non-ego personality that participates with the archetypal energies, bringing them to consciousness through personification.

Subjective Psyche: Reference to the personal interpretation or experience of consciousness.

BIBLIOGRAPHY

Adler, G., & Jaffé, Aniela, eds. *C. G. Jung Letters*. Bollingen Series XCV. Princeton, NJ: Princeton University Press, 1975.

Aitken, Robert. *Taking the Path of Zen*. San Francisco, North Point Press, 1982.

Aizenstat, Stephen. "Tending Your Dreams." Unpublished manuscript. Carpinteria, CA, 1993.

Alden, R. MacDonald. *Why the Chimes Rang*. New York: Bobbs-Merrill, 1924.

Barks, Coleman, trans. *Rumi Jelaluddin: We are Three*. Athens, GA: Maypop Books, 1987.

Beck, Walter and Francisco. *The Sacred*. Tsaile and Flagstaff, AZ: Navajo Community College Press & Northland Publishing Co., 1977.

Berry, Thomas. *The Dream of the Earth*. San Francisco: Sierra Club Books, 1988.

Bly, Robert. *The Kabir Book*. Boston: Beacon Press, 1977.

Campbell, Joseph. *Myths, Dreams and Religion*. Dallas: Spring Publications, 1970.

———. *Myths to Live By*. New York: Bantam Books, 1972.

Chinen, Allan B. *In the Ever After*. Wilmette, IL: Chiron Publications, 1989.

Colum, P. *Orpheus: Myths of the World*. New York: Macmillan, 1930.

Colum, P., Campbell, J., & Scharl, J. "The Ear of Corn," in *The Complete Grimms' Fairy Tales*. New York: Random House, 1972.

————. "The Old Man Made Young Again," in *The Complete Grimms' Fairy Tales*. New York: Random House, 1972.

Covitz, Joel. *Visions of the Night*. Boston: Shambhala. 1990.

Craighead, Meinrad. *The Litany of the Great River*. Mahwah, NJ: Paulist Press, 1991.

Dalai Lama. *Freedom in Exile: The Autobiography of the Dalai Lama*. New York: HarperCollins, 1991.

D'Aulaire, Ingri, & Edgar P. *D'Aulaires' Norse Gods and Giants*. Garden City: Doubleday, 1967.

Doty, William G. *Mythography*. Tuscaloosa, AL: University of Alabama Press, 1986.

Eisenberg, et al., eds. *Transformation of Myth through Time*. Orlando: Harcourt Brace, 1990.

Eliade, Mircea. *The Myth of the Eternal Return*. Bollingen Series XLVI. Princeton, NJ: Princeton University Press, 1954.

————. *The Quest*. Chicago: The University of Chicago Press, 1969.

————. *The Sacred & the Profane*. New York: Harcourt Brace, 1957.

Ereira, Alan, producer. *From the Heart of the World: The Elder Brothers' Warning*. New York: Mystic Fire Video, 1991.

Feng, Gia-Fu, and English, Jane. *Lao Tsu: Tao Te Ching*. New York: Vintage, division of Random House, 1972.

Green, Roger L. *King Arthur and His Knights of the Round Table*. London: Puffin Books, 1953.

Hanh, Thich Nhat. *The Miracle of Mindfulness*. Boston: Beacon Press, 1972.

————. *The Pine Gate*. Fredonia, NY: White Pine Press, 1988.

Henderson, Joseph. "Ancient Myths and Modern Man," in *Man and His Symbols*. Garden City: Doubleday, 1964.

Hobday, Sister Maria Jose. "Humming Home Your Shadow," in *Parabola*, Winter, Vol. VII, #1, 1982.

Houston, Jean. *The Search for the Beloved*. Los Angeles: J. P. Tarcher, 1987.

Jaffé, Aniela, ed. *C. G. Jung: Word and Image*. Bollingen Series XCVII. Princeton, NJ: Princeton University Press, 1979.

James, William. *The Varieties of Religious Experience*. New York: Macmillan, 1961, 1985.

Johnson, R. A. *He*. New York: HarperCollins, 1994.

———. *Inner Work*. San Francisco: HarperCollins, 1989.

Jung, C. G. *Man & His Symbols*. Garden City: Doubleday, 1964.

———. *Memories, Dreams, Reflections*. Aniela Jaffé, ed. New York: Random House, 1965, 1989.

Lang, Andrew, ed. *The Violet Fairy Book*. New York: Dover, 1966.

———. *The Yellow Fairy Book*. New York: Dover, 1966.

Leslau, C. and W. *African Folktales*. White Plains, NY: Peter Pauper Press, 1963.

Mayer, Marianna and Mercer. *Beauty and the Beast*. New York: Four Winds Press, 1978.

McMurray, M. "Amor and Psyche: A Deepening Communion," in *The Face of the Deep*. Advent Christmas Epiphany 1991–1992. Gillian Scharff, ed. Berkeley, 1991.

———. *Illuminations: The Healing Image*. Oakland: Wingbow Press, 1988.

———. "Imaginal Integrity: A Window into the Psyche," in *Psychological Perspectives*. Spring/Summer, Vol. 20, #1, 1989.

Montagnon, Peter. "The Land of the Disappearing Buddha," from the Long Search Series with Ronald Eyre. London: BBC, 1977. Time/Life films.

Moyers, Bill. "Introduction to the Power of Myth," from *Transformation of Myth through Time*, Eisenberg, et al., eds. Orlando: Harcourt Brace, 1990.

Neihardt, J. G. *Black Elk Speaks*. New York: Pocket Books, 1972.

New English Bible. New York: Cambridge University Press, 1971.

Pyle, Howard. *The Story of the Grail & the Passing of Arthur*. New York: Charles Scribner's Sons, 1933, 1985.

Reps, Paul, ed. *Zen Flesh, Zen Bones*. Boston, Rutland, Tokyo: Charles E. Tuttle, 1957.

Scholem, Gershom. *Major Trends in Jewish Mysticism*. New York: Schocken Books, 1954.

Schultz, James W. *Bear Chief's War Shirt*. Wilbur Ward Betts, ed. Missoula, MT: Mountain Press, 1984.

Seattle, Chief. "This Earth is Sacred to my People," speech delivered in 1851, reproduced by Northcoast Environmental Center, Arcata, CA.

Singer, June. *The Unholy Bible*. Boston: Sigo Press, 1986.

Sproul, Barbara C. *Primal Myths*. San Francisco: HarperSanFrancisco, 1979.

Stone, Merlin. *Ancient Mirrors of Womanhood*. Boston: Beacon Press, 1984.

Swimme, Brian. *The Universe Is a Green Dragon*. Santa Fe: Bear & Co., 1984.

Teilhard de Chardin, Pierre. *How I Believe*. New York: HarperCollins, 1969.

Trimble, S., ed. "Hopi—Wunuuqum: Ones Who Stand," in "Stories from the Land," Flagstaff, AZ: The Museum of Northern Arizona Press. *Plateau*, Vol. 53. #2, 1981.

Valley-Fox, Anne, and Keen, Sam. *Your Mythic Journey*. Los Angeles, J. P. Tarcher, 1989.

Von Franz, Marie-Louise. *C. G. Jung: His Myth in our Time*. Boston: Little Brown, 1975.

Watkins, Mary. *Waking Dreams*. Dallas: Spring Publications, 1984.

INDEX

Rain, 12
Raven, 24, 92
Remembering Myths (exercise), 23
Renaissance images, 199
Reps, Paul, 196, 197
reverence, 72
ritual, 155
Ritual and Attitude (exercise), 155

S

sacred images, 193
sacrifice, 184
sage, 199
Satan, 93
Scharff, Gillian, 50
Scharl, J., 131
Scholem, Gershom G., 23
Schultz, James Willard, 67
Seattle, Chief, 196
Self, 48, 49, 69, 84
self-reflection, 15
serpent, 35, 130
shadow
    embracing the, 103
    getting to know, 107
    Humming Home Your, 104
shamanic traditions, 184
Shiva, 93
Singer, June, 130
Sir Launcelot, 43, 44, 45
Sir Roland, 26, 27, 28, 29, 31
Siuhu, 87
snake, 18, 171
Soul, 52, 184
    development of, 2
    qualities, 65
    world, 190
Sparrow's Gift, 189
Spider Grandmother, 160, 163,
    165, 177, 179, 181, 190
Spider Woman, 190

spiritual polentials, 5
Stone, Merlin, 142
Star Woman, 82
Sproul, Barbara C., 139
Sun, 12
Swimme, Brian, 124
swordsman, 166, 177
synchronicity, 66

T

Taoism, 73
Teilhard de Chardin, Pierre, 138
temptation, 27
Tending Your Dreams, 138
Tepeu, 126
Thich Nhat Hanh, 156, 166
Touching the Whole (exercise), 136
transformation, 159
    of the ego, 43
treasure, 56
Tree of the Knowledge of Good
    and Evil, 130
Trimble, S., 161
trolls, 91
Turning Within (exercise), 49
Twin War Gods, 160, 171

U

Ugandan myth, 11
unification of opposites, 113
Universe Is a Green Dragon, 124
unseen powers, 72

V

Valley-Fox, Anne, 156

Madeline McMurray received her Ph.D. from Sierra University where her concentration was archetypal psychology. She works as a psychotherapist in private practice and lectures on topics of religious studies at Humboldt State University. With her husband, McMurray leads seminars on what it means to be living on an endangered planet. She is also an artist, writer, teacher, wife, mother and now a grandmother, and lives, as quietly as she can, with her family and dogs in the northwoods of California.